Mountain Biking
In the Bay Area

Mountain Biking In the Bay Area

Volume 1, South from San Francisco

Michael Hodgson
&
Mark Lord

Western Tanager Press
Santa Cruz

The authors have made every attempt to provide accurate information in this book, but mountain biking inevitably involves risks that cannot be foreseen. The varieties of individual human abilities, changing environmental and climatic conditions, and a range of other circumstances cannot be encompassed in any one book. Please let our book help you, but be aware that each bicyclist bears personal responsibility for his or her own safety in wilderness areas.

To our wives, Karen Samford and Sandy Lord, for soothing sore muscles, understanding muddy floors, pushing frustrated minds, and giving up their time to allow for ours. This book is truly the result of their patience.

Acknowledgements

This book is the realization of a dream that both of us have shared over the years, the dream of being authors and writing about that which we love. This book would never have seen completion without the support and guidance of many wonderful people: park rangers, friends, and loved ones. We are very indebted to the following:

The rangers and volunteers at Henry Coe State Park, especially Barry Breckling
Ranger Michael McCabe of Butano State Park
Mark and Kathleen McCarroll
Dave and Sheila Johnston
District Ranger Quinton Kay
Responsible Organized Mountain Pedalers of Campbell, CA
Stan's Bike Shop in Cupertino
Jay and Shirley Supkoff
John and Ande Clapp
John and Debbie Emerson
The Western Mountaineering folks
Bud and Norma Lord
Peter and Mary Hodgson
Tanner Girard
Doc Wanamaker
Doug Bender and Mindi Lord
Skeets, Concha, and Merritt Lord
Todd Vogel
Heidi Lord
Ranger Les Clark
National Wildlife Refuge Volunteer Monty Dewey
Publisher Hal Morris
Editor Michael Gant
Publicist Lauren Wickizer
Mapmaker Lynn Piquett

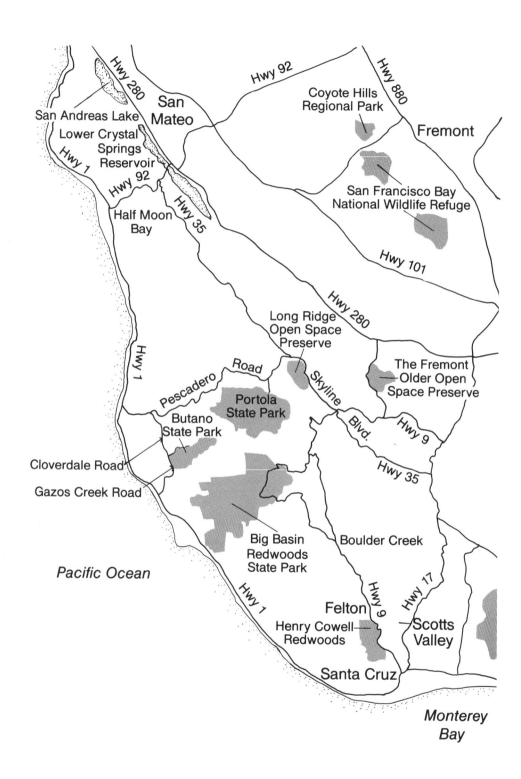

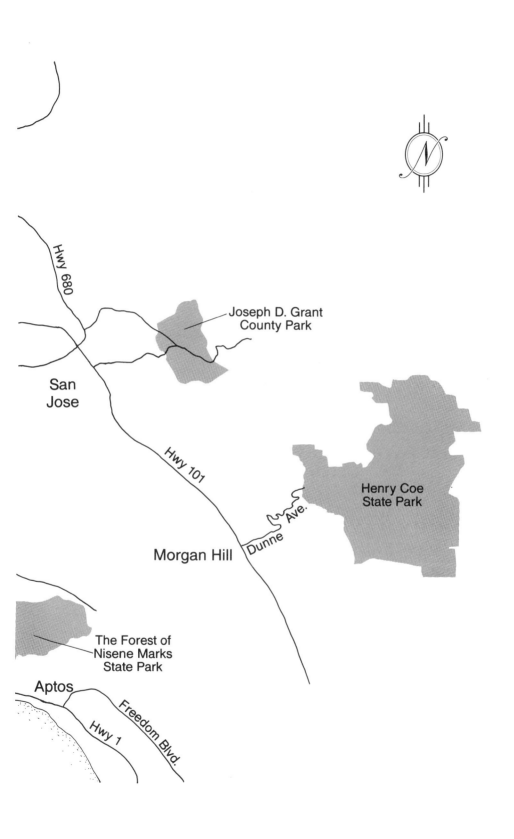

CONTENTS

Preface

It wasn't long ago that I bought my first mountain bike. Actually the bike is more correctly referred to as an All Terrain Bike, because it can go anywhere that I am willing to pedal it. Within days of my new purchase I drove to the East Bay foothills and proceeded to attack every dirt road with reckless abandon.

With sweat pouring from my body, my legs aching, my head pounding, I dismounted (collapsed) and began to wonder why I had bought a mountain bike. Suddenly, there in front of my sweat-burned eyes was my reason. A beautiful, tawny-colored bobcat was quietly watching me from not more than fifteen yards away.

The ten seconds that followed, until the bobcat faded into the trees, seemed like an eternity. It was then I realized that my mountain bike had become another excellent way for me to view the wilds. I still use my bike to achieve heart-pounding, gut-wrenching workouts, but I am ever more aware of finding time to coast quietly and listen to the world around me. Because of my bike I have been able to view far more than I ever would have dreamed possible.

The dirt roads and jeep trails that crisscross the Bay Area are the ''E Tickets'' to a backyard filled with more wonders than you've ever imagined. Take your time, ride safely, ride responsibly, have fun, and keep your eyes open. I hope you have as much fun ''discovering'' your backyard with this guide as I did researching (riding everywhere with a tape recorder and a grin pasted on my face) it for you. Happy Trails!

MICHAEL HODGSON

I recently took a close friend on her first mountain bike ride. It was a ''postcard perfect'' day, and we had spent the previous four hours riding without encountering a soul. It was difficult for either of us to believe we were only thirty minutes from a sprawling metropolis. As the day wound to a close we reluctantly dismounted our bikes and headed for home. Her ear-to-ear grin vividly brought to mind my first ride.

I had allowed myself to be coerced into a new trail "exploration" on a borrowed mountain bike. My friend excitedly explained that he knew of two fire roads and mumbled something about the vague possibility of connecting them. Several hours later, we returned happily exhausted, but without having discovered the mystery connection road. It didn't matter though, because we had experienced a world filled with wildlife and magnificent vistas that I never knew existed so close to home. We were euphoric looking back on a day spent basking in pristine meadows and "hooting" down spiraling dirt roads.

Those of us in the Bay Area are fortunate enough to be surrounded by open space, mountains, and a spectacular coast. You won't see 14,000-foot peaks or high alpine lakes, but you will find some of the finest coastal wilderness areas California has to offer. My hope in writing this guide is to present responsibly these incredibly beautiful and valuable areas that have been preserved for everyone to discover and cherish. Please help to ensure that others who follow will be able to do the same.

Ride safely, responsibly, and most importantly—enjoy!

MARK E. LORD

Introduction

Mountain biking is a much-maligned and much-loved sport. The very nature of the beast, a pedal-powered vehicle that goes virtually anywhere, is enough to thrill most adventurous souls yet send shudders down the spine of many wilderness purists.

It's not hard to imagine the shock of a hiker on a wilderness trail coming head to head (ouch) with an out-of-control mountain biker. Yet, it is also not hard to imagine the joy of quietly pedaling along a ridge by way of a jeep trail bathed in early morning light.

Both of us find tremendous pleasure in mountain biking. An all terrain bicycle in the hands of a responsible user becomes a legitimate tool for exploring the backwoods and foothills. We do not support or condone trespassing on private property or the destruction of wilderness at any time. There is more than enough land for the hiker, equestrian, and mountain biker to coexist peacefully.

In the following pages, we will take you on a journey of the Bay Area mountains and foothills. We have tried very hard to give you a sampling of the joy of mountain biking in a variety of areas. Although every ride we describe in this guide was legal at the time of printing, it is possible that any trail could be closed to mountain bikes at any time. The park services may opt to close a trail due to overuse, erosion, or political pressure. Please, if any trail or road displays this sign ⬅, even if described in this guide, respect the ruling and don't do more to ruin the image of mountain bikes by riding the trail.

Despite the rumors, encouraged in part by all the hard-core articles in newsprint, mountain biking is not just for the brave few willing to endure bone-jarring descents and breakneck speed. Mountain biking is for everyone. It is to be enjoyed at any speed, even if you find yourself discovering wild places in a way you may never have dreamed possible.

Mountain biking can be a dry-land extension of backcountry skiing, or that quiet encounter with a bobcat. It can be a morning ride through a valley shrouded in mist, or a zig-zag descent to a river swimming hole you heard about from a friend. Whatever you desire, you will find something in mountain biking for you.

It is our hope that you and your bike will experience much joy and discovery with our guide. However, this is just a starting point. There is so much more out there than we could or wanted to include. The rest is up to you.

Cyclists Code
The following is a list of "rules of conduct" for all mountain bikers to abide by. It is provided by R.O.M.P., Responsible Organized Mountain Pedalers of Campbell, California. For more information about this non-profit group call 408-356-8230 or write P.O. Box 1723, Campbell CA. 95009-1723. "Thousands of miles of dirt trails have been closed to Mountain Bicycling because of the irresponsible riding habits of a few riders. Do your part to maintain trail access by observing the following rules."

Rules of the Trail
1. RIDE ON OPEN TRAILS ONLY: Respect trail and road closures, (ask if not sure), avoid possible trespass on private land, and obtain permits and authorization as may be required. Federal and State Wilderness Areas are closed to cycling. Additional trails may be closed because of sensitive environmental concerns or conflicts with other users. Your riding example will determine what is closed to all cyclists.
2. LEAVE NO TRACE: Be sensitive to the dirt beneath you. You should not ride—even on open trails—under conditions where you will leave evidence of your passing, such as on certain soils shortly after a rain. Observe the different types of soils and trail construction and practice minimum-impact cycling. This also means staying on the trail and not creating any new ones. Be sure to pack out at least as much as you pack into an area.
3. CONTROL YOUR BICYCLE: Make known your approach well in advance. A friendly greeting (or bell) is considerate and works well; startling someone may cause loss of trail access. Show your respect when passing others by slowing to a walk or stopping altogether. Anticipate that other trail users may be around corners or blind spots.
5. NEVER SPOOK ANIMALS: All animals are startled by an unannounced approach, a sudden movement, or a loud noise. This can be dangerous for you, others, and the animals. Give animals extra room and time to adjust to you. In passing, use special care and follow the directions of horseback riders (ask if uncertain). Running cattle and disturbing

wild animals is a serious offense. Leave gates as you found them or as marked.

6. PLAN AHEAD: Know your equipment, your ability, and the area in which you are riding and prepare accordingly. Be self-sufficient at all times, keep your machine in good repair, carry necessary supplies for changes in the weather or other conditions. A well-executed trip is a satisfaction to you and not a burden or offense to others. Keep trails open by setting an example of responsible cycling for all mountain bicyclists.

Level of Difficulty Scale

Mountain biking is unique in that the same ride may appeal to beginner through advanced cyclists. Beginners may want to walk (and we do encourage walking) during those times intermediate-to-advanced riders will push their physical limits and challenge their skills. As a reminder though . . . no one should be intimidated from walking if the need arises.

BEGINNER: No off-road experience. Able to ride comfortably 10 to 20 street miles over rolling terrain.

INTERMEDIATE: Some off-road experience. Able to ride easily 20 to 40 street miles over hilly terrain. Little difficulty in controlling bike in mixed road conditions (sand, mud, loose rocks, etc.).

ADVANCED: Extensive off-road experience. Able to ride comfortably 50 or more street miles over hilly terrain and 20 to 40 miles extreme off-road conditions. No difficulty in controlling bike in mixed road conditions at a variety of speeds. Enjoys aggressively ascending or descending steep hills.

In the photo above, Michael demonstrates the proper body position for uphill riding.

Basic Biking Technique

Although power, strength and endurance have their place in mountain biking, finesse and balance are a good rider's main emphasis. Most difficult terrain and trail hazards are best maneuvered at slow speeds and in low gears. In all situations, concentrate on smooth transitions and shift gears aggressively. Anticipating upcoming gear changes is the key to successfully negotiating mountain biking's ups and downs.

UPHILL RIDING: For uphills, always start in the lowest gear; it is easier to shift up than down. Steeper hills increase the feeling of an unweighted front wheel. Compensate for this by slightly shifting your weight forward. You must be careful, however, not to unweight the rear wheel so much that you lose traction.

DOWNHILL RIDING: Descending requires finesse and balance with the added element of control. Before beginning any significant descent, lower your center of gravity by lowering your seat post one to three inches. Shift the chain to the large front sprocket as this will prevent the chain-wheel from engaging your leg should you become disengaged from the bike (only practical for extended downhill runs; rapid transitions from down to uphill require lower gearing and small sprockets). Pedals should be kept parallel to the ground with the front pedal riding slightly higher; this will prevent the pedals from catching the ground and causing an unplanned sprawl. While cornering, pedal weight should be shifted to the outside, forcing that pedal down and the inside pedal up; this will help you corner and prevents snagging your inside pedal while keeping your weight centered over the bike. Be mindful of keeping your weight on the pedals instead of the seat; it is easier to shift weight when necessary. Injuries occur most often when excessive speed causes a loss of control. Have fun, relax, and keep your head.

WATER CROSSING: Controlled momentum and keeping your weight over the seat will mean the difference between negotiating the water trap or taking a swim. It is possible to pedal steadily through up to a foot of water by avoiding large rocks, deep silt, and bad Karma.

USING YOUR BRAKES: The key to successful use of your brakes, especially when descending, is using your head. Remember that the amount of braking efficiency is directly proportional to the amount of weight (your weight) that each tire is carrying. On downhills your front wheel is carrying a majority of your weight and even more weight is transferred to your front wheel when braking. Translated, this means that your front wheel (front brake) is your "favorite pal" during downhill runs and is more likely to control your descent without going into the dreaded "locked-wheel no-control skid."

This is not to say forget your rear brake. Good riders learn to apply just enough brake pressure as is necessary for the terrain. Only practice will allow you to judge how much front and rear brake you need to provide control and avoid jackknifes, rear-wheel skids, and front-wheel lock up. Your body positioning is also important here. Ideal positioning pushes your fanny out over your rear wheel with your thighs gripping your seat. Experiment and discover what feels most comfortable to you. The more you shift your weight back over your rear wheel during downhills, the more you increase your rear wheel's braking power. Conversely, the more you shift your weight forward the more you unweight your rear wheel and the greater the opportunity you have to demonstrate a swan dive over your handlebars . . . not a pretty sight. The lesson here is to keep your weight as far back as possible. On level ground an equal use of front and rear brake is appropriate because both of your wheels are equally weighted.

In summary then: the wheel with the most weight holds the greatest braking power; on downhills, shift your weight to the rear and learn to use firm pressure on your front brake with your rear brake as support; never lock up your rear wheel on downhills.

TURNING AND DIRECTIONAL CONTROL: First tip—avoid oversteering at all costs. Second tip—relax. Many beginners and even experienced riders lock their arms and resort to the "death grip" while descending, especially when loose soil or ruts are involved. Learn to use your body and not your arms to determine direction. Keep a firm but relaxed grip on your handlebars and initiate turns by slightly twisting your shoulders into them. As you twist your shoulders, your bike will follow (skiers will recognize this technique as similar to squaring their shoulders into the fall line).

MISCELLANEOUS RIDING TIPS: Tire pressure is an important ingredient to successful traction and ease of pedaling. We recommend, depending on the tire type, soft tires (between 25 and 40 psi, not mushy, but soft to the squeeze of thumb and forefingers) for sandy and loose terrain. For firm terrain and hard ground, again depending on the tire type, higher pressure is the norm (between 35 and 50 psi, resistant to squeezing between thumb and forefinger, but not rock-hard). Use caution when riding on soft tires as you are more likely to damage your rim and become the victim of pinched tire flats.

Pedaling through deep sand is exhausting and technically difficult. This is one of those situations when your bike knows best. Relax and let the bike somewhat steer itself. Hold your momentum upon approach and entry. Downshift as low as is necessary without expending too much energy.

During downhill runs learn to "bunny hop" your front wheel over ruts, washouts, potholes, and other small unavoidable obstacles.

For energy conservation, use "revolutionary" pedaling, when possible. While pushing down with one pedal utilize your toe clips and pull up with the other pedal. This offers you increased power and efficiency.

Keep your bike clean after rides. Accumulated dust and grit on the chain, cables, and gears encourages increased wear and tear and untimely equipment failure.

STRETCHING: The majority of biking injuries can be alleviated by stretching muscles before and after riding. Jumping onto your bike without a warm-up is very hard on your body, regardless of physical condition. Besides, a general five-to-ten-minute stretching program will also do wonders for your riding ability. Pay particularly close attention to stretching thigh and calf muscles; lower, mid-, and upper back; and neck muscles. Think of the minutes spent as insurance against months of recuperation caused by injury.

Chapter One
SAN ANDREAS
AND SAWYER CAMP TRAILS

TOPO: *San Mateo 7.5' and Montara Mountain 7.5'*
THE RIDE: *Beginner and Above*
MILEAGE: *16.5*

Description

Located in San Mateo County alongside San Andreas Lake and Lower Crystal Springs Reservoir, San Andreas and Sawyer Camp trails are two of the most popular trails in the midcounty trail system. The valley that these two trails run through is known as the San Francisco Watershed. This valley has been formed over the years partly by sinking of land within the San Andreas Fault zone and partly by stream erosion in the "crush" zone of the fault.

This particular area is very rich in anthropological and human history. Home for many thousands of years to the Shalshone Indians, this land also became a stopping point for Gaspar de Portolá and his men in 1769. In 1774 Captain Rivera, an officer in Portolá's party, further explored the Peninsula, camping near what is now known as Jepson Laurel. Jepson Laurel is one of the most famous landmarks on the Sawyer Camp Trail and, at over six hundred years of age, is the oldest and largest laurel in California.

The land, bought in later years by Leander Sawyer, was used for grazing cattle. The trail running through here was once the main highway from San Francisco to Half Moon Bay. When the City of San Francisco took over the land around 1888, it fenced in the road to protect San Francisco's drinking water.

9

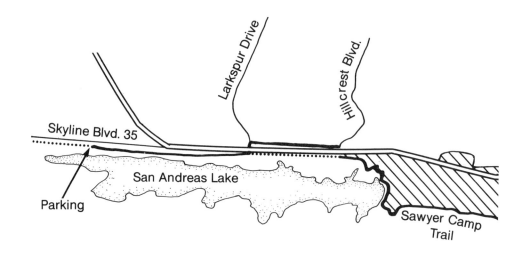

SAN ANDREAS
AND SAWYER CAMP TRAILS

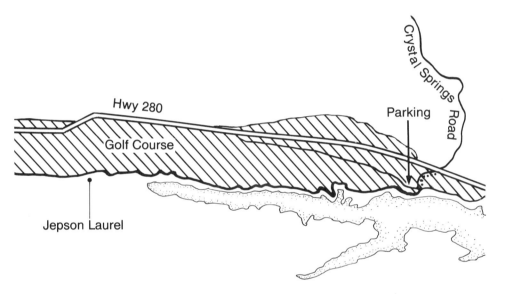

In 1978, San Mateo County designated the road a recreational trail and paved it for bicycles with money from the State Department of Parks and Recreation.

Getting There

From Daly City and farther north, park at the northernmost point of the San Andreas Trail. From Highway 280 north take Skyline Boulevard for approximately .25 mile south of San Bruno Avenue. Parking is at the signed trail entrance on the west side of the road. From 280 south take Sneath Lane and go south on the frontage road to San Bruno. Turn right on San Bruno Avenue to Skyline Boulevard, where you will turn left and drive about .25 mile to the parking area.

From the south, park at the southernmost point for Sawyer Camp Trail. From 280 north, exit Highway 92 west to Half Moon Bay. Turn right (north) on Skyline Boulevard. Drive about 1.5 miles to Crystal Springs Road. Parking is along Skyline Boulevard just past the trail entrance (on the west side) and the intersection with Crystal Springs Road.

The Ride

Whether you start at the north and ride south, or start at the south and ride north, the ride is an easy and enjoyable out-and-back journey for all levels. It is perhaps a little easier to begin the ride from the south because the 400 feet of elevation gain is gradually accomplished in the beginning and the ride is all downhill or level from then on.

Beginning at the Crystal Springs entrance, ride north on the paved Sawyer Camp Trail. At about 3 miles the trail crosses San Andreas Creek where it feeds into the Lower Crystal Springs Reservoir. About 1 mile beyond the creek you will pass by Jepson Laurel, named after Willis Jepson, noted 1920s California botanist. At about 5 miles the trail will begin to climb gradually from San Andreas Lake and the dam up to Skyline Boulevard. If you wish to cut your ride short, you can turn around here and your round-trip mileage will be 12 miles.

If you wish to continue on, you will need to ride about .8 mile of the east frontage road between Hillcrest Boulevard and Larkspur Drive. The present section of connecting trail between San Andreas Trail and Sawyer Camp Trail is not open to bicycles. Cross under Highway 280 on Hillcrest and turn left on the frontage road. Turn right on Larkspur Drive and join the San Andreas Trail ''already in progress.'' Pedal another 1.5 miles to the trail end and turn around for the return trip back to your car. Although

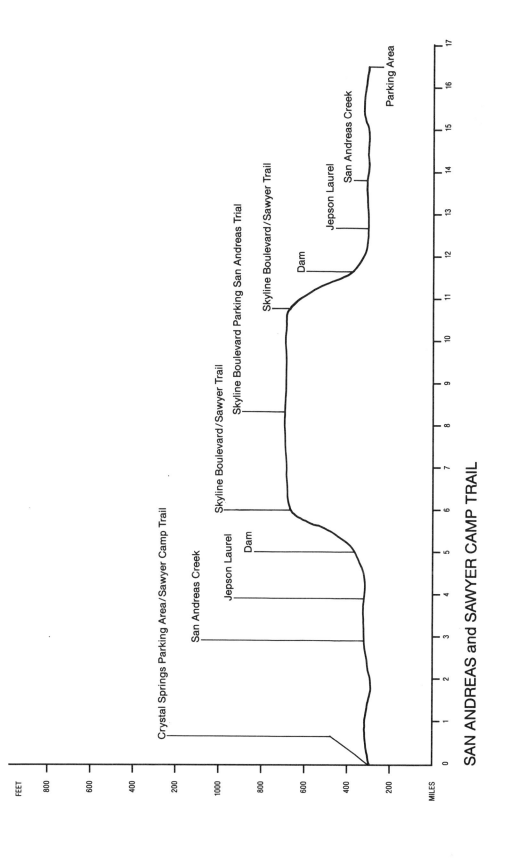

SAN ANDREAS and SAWYER CAMP TRAIL

the freeway is very close on this last section, the views of the surrounding landscape and the proximity of a sparkling lake make this a most enjoyable addition.

Chapter Two
PORTOLA STATE PARK

TOPO: *La Honda 7.5' and Mindego Hill 7.5'*
THE RIDE: *Beginner and Above*
MILEAGE: *12.7*

Description

Portola State Park is a 2,400-acre evergreen forest set in the rugged land-scape of the northwestern Santa Cruz Mountains. The park is named after the Spanish explorer Don Gasper de Portolá, who led an expedition in 1769 through the area in search of anchorage for his boats. Later, because of the incredible demand for timber during and after the California Gold Rush, the Portola area was subjected to heavy logging in the late 1800s. It wasn't until 1945 that the State of California acquired 1,600 acres for use as a park. The additional 800 acres of land were donated by the Save-the-Redwoods League during subsequent years.

In addition to the Portola acreage, the development of an adjoining 7,000-plus acres of Pescadero Creek County Park allows the visitor a unique experience among the towering coastal redwoods and Douglas firs. Rushing streams, dense ferns, and open meadows provide the backdrop for this magnificent forest.

Getting There

Portola State Park is located just a few miles southeast of La Honda in the Santa Cruz Mountains. One of the easiest ways to get to Portola is south on Alpine Road off Highway 35. To get there from San Jose take Highway 9; from Palo Alto take Page Mill Road; from Redwood City and points north take Highway 84. Once on Alpine Road you will drive approximately 3 miles to the turnoff onto Portola State Park Road. Be careful

15

PESCADERO
COUNTY PARK

Pescadero Road

Memorial Park

Old Haul Road

Butano Ridge Loop Trail

PORTOLA STATE PARK

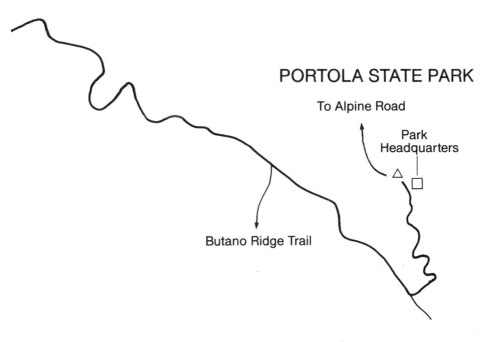

PORTOLA STATE PARK

To Alpine Road

Park
Headquarters

Butano Ridge Trail

here as the next 4 miles to the parking area and park headquarters are a very narrow and winding descent. Park your car and begin your ride.

The Ride

This ride is extremely well suited for all levels of mountain bikers. Beginning at the park headquarters, pedal down the road, cross the bridge and bear right at the junction towards the group picnic shelter, approximately .25 mile. Go through the service road gate and continue another .75 mile to Iverson Cabin and the park employee residences. Service vehicles occasionally use the road to this point, so be very careful and be ready to yield at any time. From Iverson Cabin you must walk your bike about 200 yards to the gate and boundary with Pescadero Creek County Park. At the gate you will turn right onto Old Haul Road for a rolling but moderate ride to Memorial County Park and Pescadero Road. Once you reach Old Haul Road Trailhead and parking area, turn around and pedal back the way you came.

You will have every bit as much fun going back as you did getting here. The road is wide enough and moderate enough that a little speed offers minimal risks and maximum fun. As always, yield to hikers and equestrians. Round trip from the gate at Portola onto Old Haul Road and back is approximately 10 miles. Your total mileage round trip back to the parking area is approximately 12.7 miles. Starting elevation is 400 feet, climbing to 800 feet midway to Memorial Park and descending back to 400 feet. Have Fun!

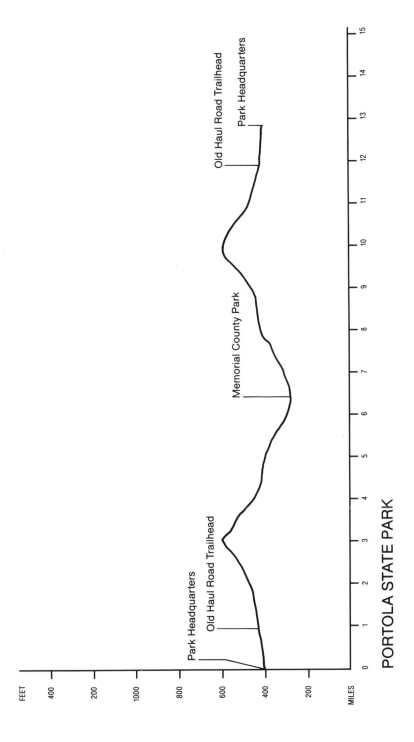

PORTOLA STATE PARK

Chapter Three
BUTANO STATE PARK

TOPO: *Franklin Point 7.5'*
RIDE #1: *Beginner and Above with a park ranger escort only*
MILEAGE: *11.5*
RIDE #2: *Intermediate and Above with an option for overnight*
MILEAGE: *13*

Description

Nestled in the Santa Cruz Mountains of southern San Mateo County lies Butano State Park, a 2,200-acre redwood preserve. In the language of the Ohlone Indian, Butano means roughly "gathering place of friendly people." This park is named because the area was the spring and summer commerce and social gathering center of the Ohlone. Logging the coastal redwood for shingles was big industry in this valley in the mid-1800s. The operation threatened to eliminate virtually all of the virgin redwood until, through a series of fluke circumstances, the logging mill's final owner committed suicide and all logging ceased. Little Butano Valley was saved, and one can now view excellent examples of coastal redwood. Although the area was considered for purchase as a park in the 1950s, it wasn't until 1961 that the park was finally dedicated.

Getting There

Located between Half Moon Bay and Santa Cruz off Highway 1. Coming from Half Moon Bay, drive 14 miles from the last stop light on Highway 1 to Pescadero Road. Turn left and continue 2.25 miles to Cloverdale Road and turn right. Drive 5.5 miles to the park entrance on the left side. Coming from Santa Cruz, drive approximately 25 miles north on Highway 1 to Cloverdale Road, where you turn right. Continue 3 miles to the signed

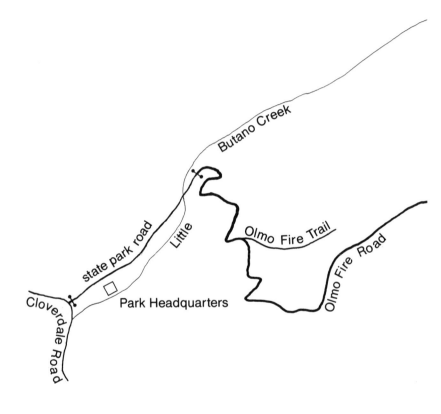

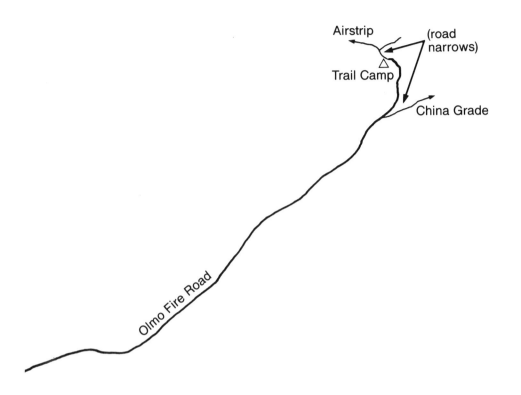

Airstrip (road narrows)

Trail Camp

China Grade

Olmo Fire Road

BUTANO STATE PARK

park entrance on your right. Parking may be found either at the entrance gate or at the picnic area.

The Ride

Sandy hills and severe altitude gains make the self-guided rides in Butano suitable only for intermediates and above. If you consider yourself a hardy beginner, the scenic beauty is well worth the effort, although you will find yourself walking your bike a lot — you may even wonder why you brought it along at times.

Ride #1

Perhaps the most scenic and certainly most gentle ride can only be done with a park ranger as guide. Riders of all levels will enjoy and appreciate this unique park-sponsored mountain bike ride. Ranger Michael McCabe designed this combination mountain bike ride and park interpretive program to promote responsible use of park lands and allow access into beautiful, but previously unaccessible, private holdings. The rides are held on weekends during the summer months only, and space must be reserved in advance at 415-879-0173 due to the popularity.

The ride winds gradually uphill for approximately 5.5 miles through dense stands of redwoods and Douglas fir, affording spectacular views (weather permitting) of the surrounding mountains and ocean. At the midsection the ride is mostly level for approximately 1 mile to allow time to get ready for the final 5-mile rapid descent. In addition to abundant wildlife, the periodic natural and anthropologic information shared by the ranger/guide makes this a don't-miss opportunity. Please remember, since this particular ride crosses private land, it is only allowed when accompanied by a ranger.

Ride #2

While this ride can certainly be enjoyed as a day trip, we are recommending it as an overnight possibility. The midway or turnaround point, Butano Trail Camp, is 6.5 miles from the park entrance and approximately 1,200 feet of elevation gain. Butano Trail Camp is a primitive trail camp with six sites that must be reserved in advance. Each site has space for a tent. No fires are allowed, there is a pit toilet, and you must bring in your own water at the present time.

Beginning at the entrance gate, pedal approximately .5 mile on fairly level, paved road to the service gate for Olmo Fire Trail, where you turn right. The road turns rough and eventually to gravel as it winds its way steeply upward gaining 720 feet in just over a mile. Shortly after gaining relatively level ground you will notice a fire road branching off to the right.

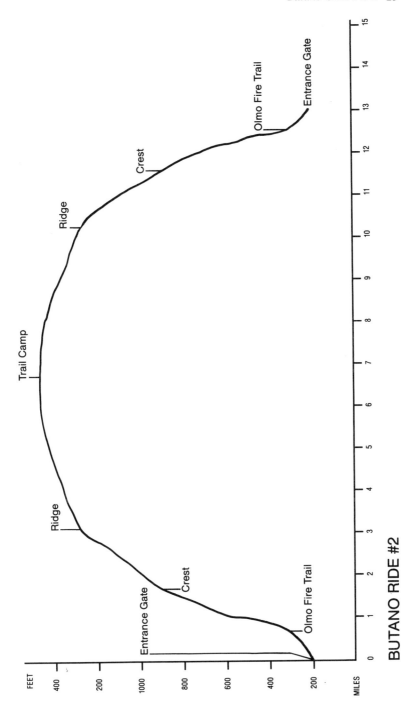

BUTANO RIDE #2

Turn right on the Olmo Fire Road, gaining another 400 feet of elevation over the next mile. As the trail opens up onto a sandy ridge you may wish to dismount and walk your bike — the next mile gains 500 very sandy feet. Take your time, enjoy the view and the small consolation that the return trip is much more fun.

As the ridge trail disappears back into the woods, and firmer ground, keep a sharp eye out for a left turn to the Butano Trail Camp. The access from Olmo Fire Road is narrow, like single track, so watch your speed. Once camp is set up, it is worth a short pedal .75 mile up the Butano Fire Trail to an old landing strip and excellent vistas. Do not proceed any farther than the landing strip with your mountain bike, as you will be trespassing on private land. The return trip is an "E ticket" ride back the way you came to the entrance gate and your car. Please watch your speed — others use the trail too.

Chapter Four
BIG BASIN STATE PARK

TOPO: *Big Basin 7.5'; Año Nuevo 7.5'; Franklin Point 7.5'*
RIDE #1: *Strong Intermediate and Above with an option for overnight*
MILEAGE: *16.5*
RIDE #2: *Intermediate and Above*
MILEAGE: *19.5 to bus or 13.5 with car shuttle*
RIDE #3: *Beginner and Above*
MILEAGE: 10.4

Description
Located in Santa Cruz County, Big Basin Redwoods State Park encompasses over 16,000 acres of some of the world's most beautiful and majestic redwoods. These trees have witnessed more than 1,000 years of man's transition: Ohlone Indians passing through in reverence and awe, the Portolá expedition of 1769 camping at Waddell Creek, the lumber mills of 1862, and Big Basin's inception as a park in 1902.

At present the park boasts over 100 miles of hiking trails, 188 campsites, a museum and nature center, and a combination campstore, gift shop, and snack bar. Although all of the single-track trails are closed to mountain bikes, there are still miles of service road and fire road to be explored. Bring your sense of wonder and adventure and enjoy this park to the fullest.

Getting There
From Highway 9 and Boulder Creek, just north of Santa Cruz, drive 9 miles north on Highway 236. From Highway 9 off Highway 35 coming from Palo Alto or points north, drive approximately 8 miles south on

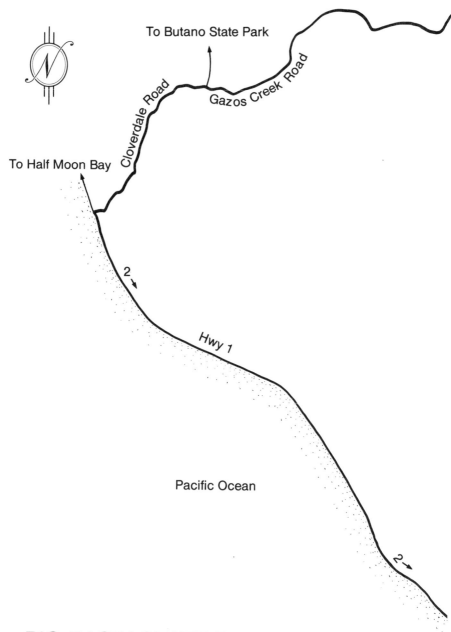

To Butano State Park

Cloverdale Road

Gazos Creek Road

To Half Moon Bay

2

Hwy 1

Pacific Ocean

2

BIG BASIN STATE PARK

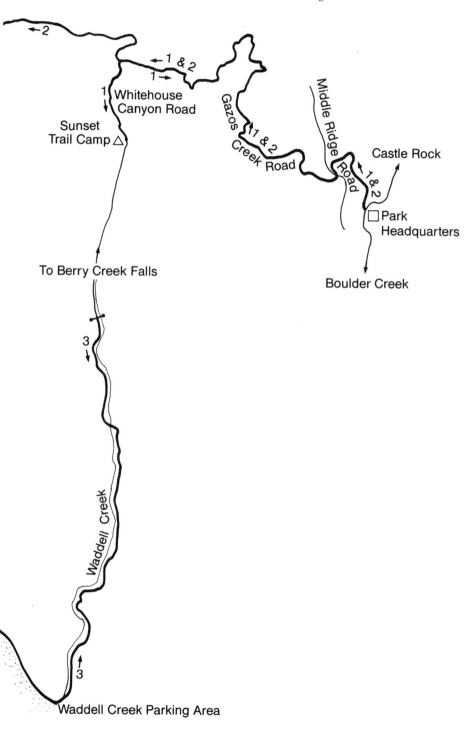

← 2

← 1 & 2

1 →

1
↓

Whitehouse
Canyon Road

Gazos Creek Road

1 & 2

Middle Ridge Road

1 & 2

Castle Rock

Sunset
Trail Camp △

□ Park
Headquarters

To Berry Creek Falls

Boulder Creek

3
↓

Waddell Creek

3
↑

Waddell Creek Parking Area

Highway 236. Leave your vehicle at the park entrance/headquarters day-use parking area.

The Ride

Big Basin offers numerous fire roads for mountain bike exploration. Check at the park headquarters for current trail status. We have selected three rides. One is an overnighter for strong riders; one a shuttle or bus trip to the coast, also for strong riders; the last an excellent out-and-back streamside pedal for any level. These rides provide a broad representation of the park's offerings. We do, however, encourage legal exploration on your own. Check with the park headquarters for other options.

Ride #1

Beginning at the park headquarters and 1,000-foot elevation, ride approximately .5 mile north on Highway 236 to the Gazos Creek Road turnoff. Bear left to the gate and continue 1.3 miles on easy terrain gaining 320 feet to the intersection with Middle Ridge Road. Continue on Gazos Creek Road, losing approximately 500 feet elevation in 2 miles. The descent is easy and fun, but sharp and blind corners require controlled speed. Near the end of the downhill a gate will be encountered—another reason to remain in control. Beyond the gate the riding becomes somewhat difficult due to very silty conditions combined with a steady climb.

After 3 miles of this challenging terrain, Whitehouse Canyon will be encountered (6.5 miles from headquarters and elevation 1,350 feet); bear left and pedal a fairly level .5 mile to another gate and the turnoff for Sunset Trail Camp. The ride drops quickly, losing 350 feet in just under a mile. The road is rutted, so watch your speed. There are 10 sites here, all primitive and requiring reservations. Campstoves are required and you must provide your own water. Pit toilets are provided. Retrace your path to your car and the park headquarters for a total roundtrip mileage of approximately 16.5 miles.

Ride #2

This ride involves either a car shuttle or a bus return to Big Basin. For the car shuttle you will need to leave one car at the intersection of Gazos Creek Road and Cloverdale Road. There is a small dirt parking area available. The bus return requires having to pedal 6 miles on Highway 1 to Waddell Beach for the bus pickup. (Call Santa Cruz Metro Bus Distict at 408-425-8600 for bus schedule and route #.)

This trip begins at the Big Basin Park Headquarters and follows Ride #1's description until Whitehouse Canyon Road. From the Whitehouse Canyon Road turnoff, continue straight on Gazos Creek Road. It is all

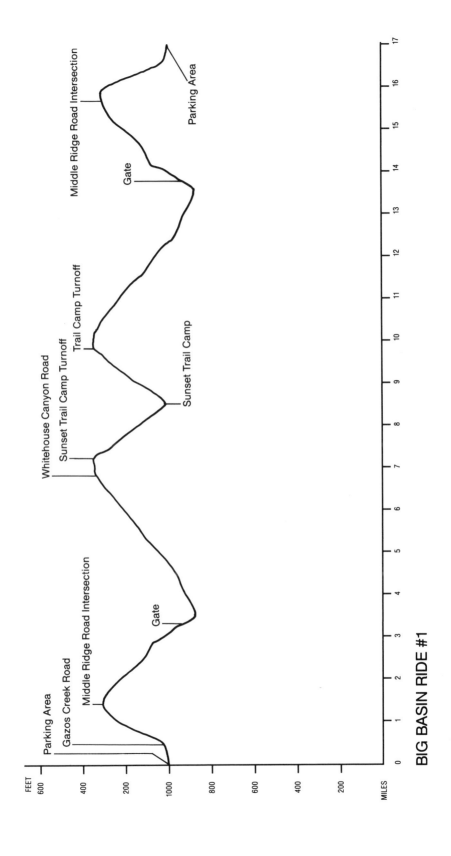

BIG BASIN RIDE #1

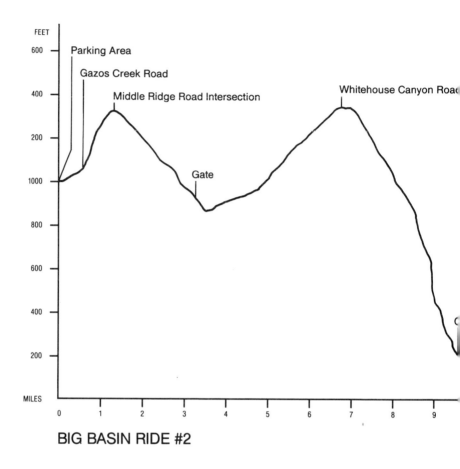

BIG BASIN RIDE #2

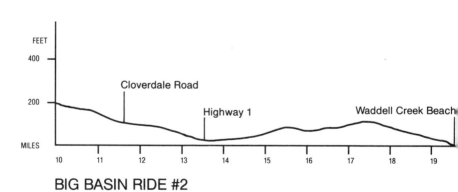

BIG BASIN RIDE #2

downhill from here, 5 miles of downhill to be exact. The road is rough and used by logging trucks, so ride with caution. At about mile 3 during the descent, and approximately 200 feet elevation, you will encounter a gate over which you will have to lift your bike. The remaining 2 miles are relatively flat leading out to Cloverdale Road and your car if you are doing a shuttle. If you are continuing on with the bus option, turn left on Cloverdale Road and pedal about 2 miles out to Highway 1. Turn left (south) on Highway 1 for a challenging 6-mile ride to Waddell Beach bus stop — challenging because of the number and speed of cars whizzing by every few seconds. Do Be Very Careful! Take the bus back to Santa Cruz, where you will change buses to Big Basin and your car.

Ride #3

This ride begins and ends at the Waddell Beach Parking Area just off Highway 1 north of Santa Cruz and is perfect for all levels of riders. The ride is extremely scenic. Should you wish to turn this into an overnight, there are a number of trail camps along the way that are open to bicycles (contact Big Basin for reservations). From the parking area, pedal approximately 5.2 miles of relatively smooth and level dirt road to the trailhead for Berry Creek Falls.

This is as far as you can and will want to go with your bike; the falls, however, are well worth the visit. If you have a lock, leave your bike and hike the falls, 2 miles round trip. Return the way you came. There is one stream crossing that gives you an option of using the bridge or crashing through the stream. If you are feeling adventurous and want to try your skills at stream crossing, downshift and go for it. Remember to keep your momentum going at a steady pace and keep your weight over your pedals. Wahoo!

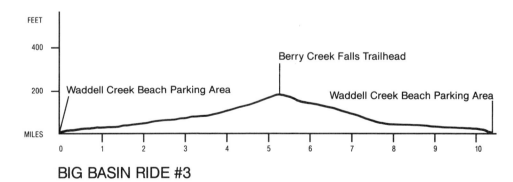

BIG BASIN RIDE #3

Chapter Five
LONG RIDGE
OPEN SPACE PRESERVE

TOPO: *Mindego Hill 7.5'*
THE RIDE: *Beginner and Above*
MILEAGE: *7.6*

Description
Managed by the Midpeninsula Open Space District, Long Ridge Open Space Preserve is a wonderful playground for hikers, bikers, and equestrians. This preserve offers some excellent opportunities to enjoy legal single-track mountain biking. Dedicated to managing the balanced use of recreation and environmental protection, Long Ridge Open Space features much in the way of shaded forest, oak-studded meadows, winding trails, and magnificent views.

As you enjoy the area observe the tree stumps, abandoned orchards, and open grassland that may once have been used as hay fields by homesteaders in the late 1860s. Since you will be riding on single track, watch your speed and control; others use the trails too. Be sure to pack a picnic lunch or take some time to pause on the open ridges overlooking the Santa Cruz Mountains—the views are spectacular.

Getting There
Located on Highway 35 midway between Page Mill Road (to the north) and Saratoga Gap and Highway 9 (to the south). Parking is provided on either side of Highway 35 and the trailheads for Long Ridge Open Space and Grizzly Flat.

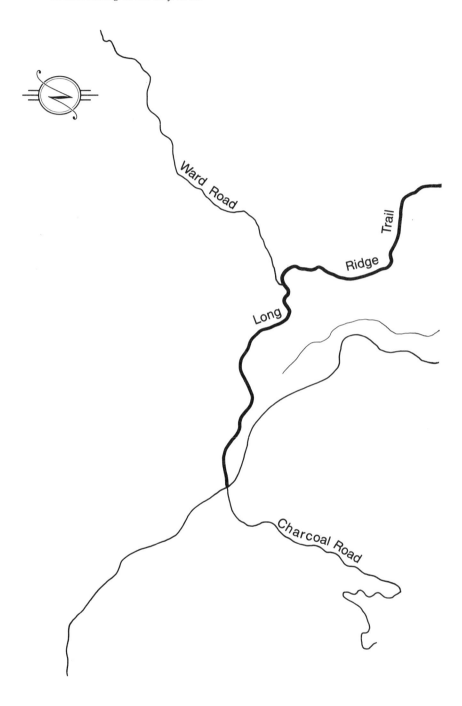

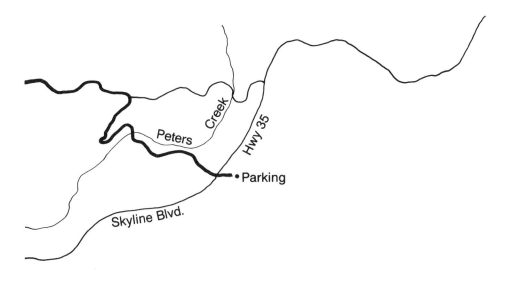

△ Table Mountain

LONG RIDGE OPEN SPACE PRESERVE

The Ride

Round trip is approximately 7.6 miles and suitable for all levels of riders. Begin on the south side of Highway 35 and the trailhead for Long Ridge/Peters Creek Trail. Descend .4 mile on single track with a few sharp turns to a stream crossing and the intersection of the Long Ridge and Peters Creek Trail. Bear left and parallel along the stream towards the Long Ridge Trail. As the terrain opens into a meadow, stay alert. You will want to bear right and pedal up the ridge approximately 150 yards after entering the meadow. If you continue straight and miss the turn, you will encounter barbed wire and a large chain across the trail. This is private property.

From the meadow, the trail widens into fire road and climbs gently to a hairpin turn and the intersection with Long Ridge Trail. It is approximately 1.3 miles from the trailhead to this point. Head left and up onto more single track. This single track will take you up another .9 mile of sharply winding trail to the ridge. Bear left on the fire road and pedal another .5 mile to the intersection of Long Ridge Trail and Ward Road. Continue on Long Ridge another 1.1 rolling miles until you reach its intersection with Highway 35. Turn around and ride back the way you came. Keep in mind that this time you will be descending much of the single track you came up and that it is heavily used by hikers and other bikers; watch your speed and be courteous.

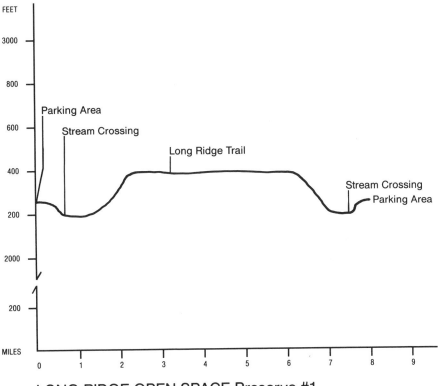

LONG RIDGE OPEN SPACE Preserve #1

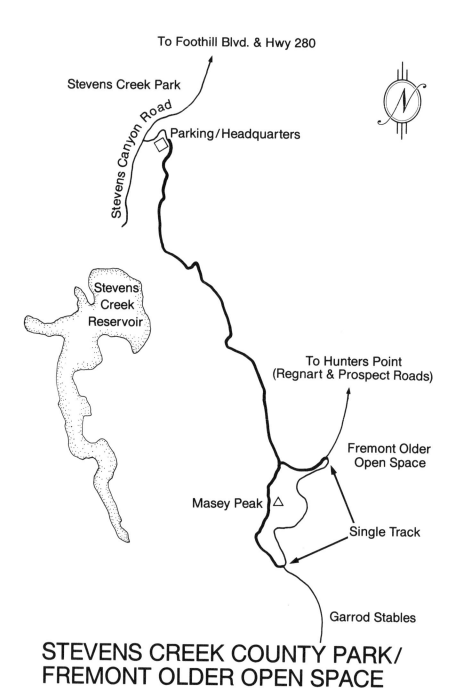

To Foothill Blvd. & Hwy 280

Stevens Creek Park

Stevens Canyon Road

Parking / Headquarters

Stevens Creek Reservoir

To Hunters Point
(Regnart & Prospect Roads)

Fremont Older
Open Space

Masey Peak

Single Track

Garrod Stables

STEVENS CREEK COUNTY PARK/
FREMONT OLDER OPEN SPACE

Chapter Six
STEVENS CREEK COUNTY PARK
FREMONT OLDER OPEN SPACE

TOPO: *Cupertino 7.5'*
THE RIDE: *Beginner and Above*
MILEAGE: *4.5*

Description
Beginning in Stevens Creek County Park, the oldest county park in the system, and passing through Fremont Older Open Space, this ride offers the biker/hiker a unique escape from the nearby surrounding urban sprawl. Although the old wineries and late-18th-century settlements have long since disappeared, this area still maintains a unique blend of natural and anthropological history. Use caution on the trails, which are heavily traveled by hikers, bikers, and equestrians (there are several major stables nearby).

Getting There
Take the Foothill Boulevard exit off of Highway 280 and head south. In approximately 3 miles Foothill turns into Stevens Canyon Road. Turn left into the park headquarters/visitor center parking area. Leave your car and head toward the trailhead for Old Canyon Trail, which begins by the visitor center.

The Ride
Beginning at the visitor center parking area, pedal .2 mile to the trailhead for the Old Canyon Trail (actually a fire road which branches off to the left). Follow the fire road .3 mile on fairly level ground to the intersection with Rim Trail. Bear left and begin climbing. After about .6 mile and 400

41

feet of elevation gain you will pedal past a trail branching off toward your left. Keep heading straight and up. Soon you will pass by private property on your left and a large water tank. Approximately .6 mile after the last trail intersection turn left onto the cutoff trail for Regnart and Prospect roads. You will descend 160 feet in a little under .4 mile to encounter another trail branching off to your right.

While our guided ride follows this single track to the right, you do have the option of adding approximately 1.3 miles to your trip by heading left and out to Hunters Point and back. Hunters Point overlooks the bay and affords the visitor a pretty view of the city below and Moffet Field. Either way you will end up on the single track pedaling towards Garrod Stables. Follow the single track through one intersection, with trails branching right and left, straight and slightly up until you once again meet up with the fire road .8 mile later. Turn right and pedal approximately .3 mile to Masey Peak, elevation 1,160 feet. From Masey Peak it is another .4 mile downhill to the cutoff, now on your right, for Prospect and Regnart roads. From here, retrace your path back to the parking area and your car. Round-trip mileage is approximately 4.5 miles.

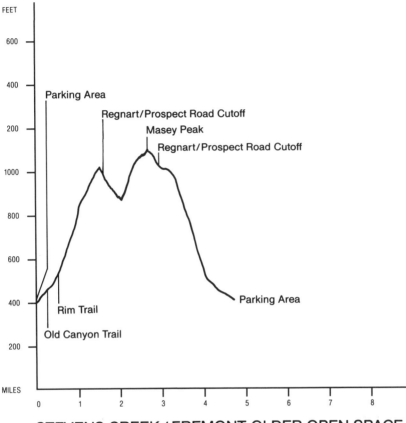

FEET

600

400

Parking Area

Regnart/Prospect Road Cutoff

200

Masey Peak

Regnart/Prospect Road Cutoff

1000

200

Parking Area

400

Rim Trail

Old Canyon Trail

200

MILES

0   1   2   3   4   5   6   7   8

STEVENS CREEK / FREMONT OLDER OPEN SPACE

Chapter Seven
HENRY COWELL STATE PARK

TOPO: *Felton 7.5'*
THE RIDE: *Advanced Beginners and Above*
MILEAGE: *9*

Description
Henry Cowell State Park is a fine ride offering a variety of terrain and climate zones, a rare vista of the Santa Cruz Mountains and the coastline, and an exciting crossing of the San Lorenzo River. Originally inhabited by Zayante Indians over 200 years ago, this area has changed little. The beauty and solitude of this land were first protected by Henry Cowell, a prominent landowner in 1860, and later the parcel was combined with an additional 1,500 acres and gift-deeded to the State of California by his son in 1954. While the park is best known for its giant coast redwood trees, it is also popular with swimmers and fishermen, the latter testing their skills against steelhead and silver salmon from mid-November to the end of February.

Getting There
Just off Highway 9, five miles north of Santa Cruz, and 1 mile south of Felton. From Highway 17 take Mount Hermon Road 3 miles west to Graham Hill Road. Turn right and continue .5 mile to Highway 9 in the town of Felton. Turn left on Highway 9 and head south 1 mile to the day-use entrance of the Henry Cowell State Park. Turn left into the park and follow the main road to the concession lot, where you will leave your car.

The Ride
Just south of the concession-area parking is the start of your ride. Follow

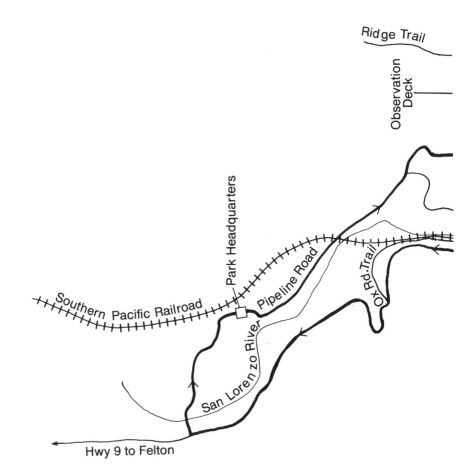

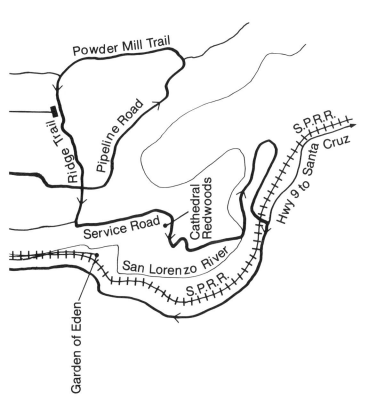

HENRY COWELL STATE PARK

the service road past Redwood Grove to the trailhead for Pipeline Road. Turn left onto the paved Pipeline Road, pedaling under dense canopy for approximately .6 mile to the underpass of the Roaring Camp Railway Line. Shortly after that, and just past the Eagle Creek trail intersection, a rather strenuous climb commences. Beginners may wish to walk until the sharp rise crests at the Ridge Trail junction. Continue straight on Pipeline Road, over rolling terrain with excellent vistas to your right of San Lorenzo Valley and brief glimpses of the ocean. After pedaling approximately 2.2 miles, bear left at Powder Mill Trail.

Powder Mill ascends, steeply at times, to its junction with the Ridge Trail. You will pass several trails branching to your right that lead to the park campground. During the climb beware of numerous sand traps. At the junction to the Ridge Trail you will bear left and up to the Observation Deck, a much-needed rest, and an excellent lunch spot. From the deck enjoy great views of the surrounding area, including Monterey Bay and Santa Cruz to the south. If you are lucky enough to plan your ride after a rain, you will be rewarded with haze-free vistas that stretch as far as the eye can see.

Intermediate-to-advanced riders looking for a bit of adventure can descend the Ridge Trail .5 mile to Pipeline Road. Watch your speed and control; the trail is very sandy and becomes difficult to maneuver over some of the steep drops and bumps. Beginners and those feeling less adventurous will turn around at the Observation Deck and retrace the route along Powder Mill Trail and back onto Pipeline Road to the Ridge Trail intersection. (To continue on the Ridge Trail down from Pipeline Road requires a river crossing. If, after checking with the ranger station, you discover that the San Lorenzo River is at high water, head back down the Pipeline Road to the concession area and your car. This is also a great option for someone who is tired and wishes to shorten the ride.) From the intersection, cross the Pipeline Road and pedal .2 mile on the Ridge Trail over easy terrain to the intersection with Rincon Trail.

At the Rincon Trail/Service Road junction, bear left on the service road; riders are reminded to stay off Rincon Trail, which parallels the road. Pedal .6 gradually descending mile to Cathedral Redwoods, where it is well worth dismounting and taking time to enjoy the magical splendor. After resting, the ride begins its glorious and occasionally steep descent (lower your seat post for this one!) to the San Lorenzo River. Near the bottom of the valley, the trail forks. Stay left and follow the high road; the trail is in better condition and will take you to a more direct crossing of the river.

Kick your shoes off and enjoy the swimming holes. When ready, hoist your bike and wade to the trail junction on the opposite side. Follow the service road up a steep climb (beginners may want to walk) approximately .5 mile to a railway crossing and Highway 9/Rincon Trail parking area. Turn right onto Highway 9 and follow the winding road 3 miles back to the entrance of the park. Turn right onto the entrance road and go another .5 mile to the concession parking area and your car.

On your ride up Highway 9 be cautious of traffic. You might be interested in a short .5-mile jaunt down to Ox Trail, which branches off to the right from Highway 9 at 1.5 miles. There is some decent rock scrambling and swimming to be had in the Garden of Eden at the end of the trail. You will lose about 300 feet in elevation; keep in mind you will have to pedal back up.

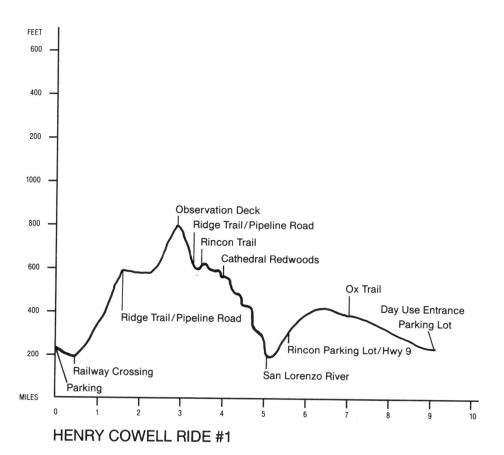

HENRY COWELL RIDE #1

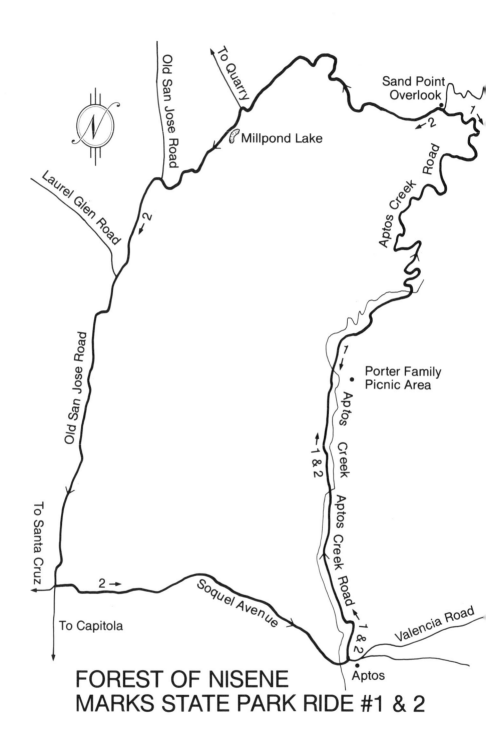

To Quarry

Old San Jose Road

Sand Point
Overlook

← 2

↙ 1

Aptos Creek Road

Laurel Glen Road

← 2

🐾 Millpond Lake

N

Old San Jose Road

↑ 1

Porter Family
Picnic Area

Aptos Creek

← 1 & 2

Aptos Creek Road

To Santa Cruz

2 →

Soquel Avenue

← 1 & 2

Valencia Road

To Capitola

↑ 1 & 2

Aptos

FOREST OF NISENE
MARKS STATE PARK RIDE #1 & 2

Chapter Eight
FOREST OF NISENE MARKS STATE PARK

TOPO: *Soquel 7.5'; Laurel 7.5'; Loma Prieta 7.5'; Watsonville West 7.5'*
RIDE #1: *Intermediate and Above*
MILEAGE: *18*
RIDE #2: *Intermediate and Above*
MILEAGE: *24*
RIDE #3: *Advanced Only!*
MILEAGE: *29.5*

Description

Today's visitor to the lush surroundings of Nisene Marks State Park will have difficulty imagining the extensive clear cutting and wanton destruction that occurred during heavy logging in the late 19th and early 20th centuries. Fortunately, 9,600 acres were purchased by the Marks family in 1950. With assistance from the Nature Conservancy, the property was donated in 1963 to the State of California. This donation was made under the condition that the natural process of restoration would continue. Much of what you see today is second growth. Even the existence of what was once a small, bustling town is a distant memory and difficult to picture.

This park is a growing tribute to a forest's regenerative capability and, as stated in the State Park's brochure, "It is a forest in a state of becoming." The Forest of Nisene Marks boasts over 30 miles of hiking trails and fire roads for public use. Due to erosion and very narrow trails, mountain bikers are restricted to fire roads. Please remember, as always, you are sharing the trails with hikers and equestrians.

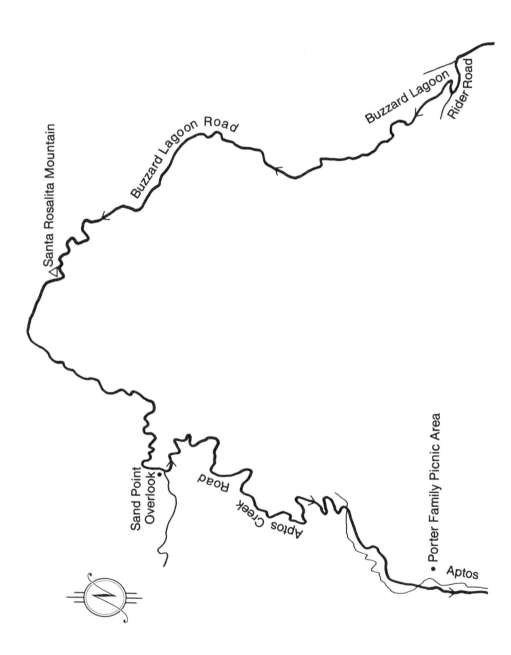

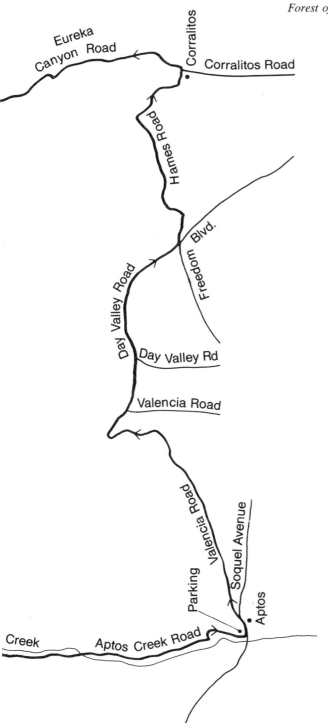

Eureka
Canyon Road

Corralitos

Corralitos Road

Hames Road

Freedom Blvd.

Day Valley Road

Day Valley Rd

Valencia Road

Valencia Road

Soquel Avenue

Parking

Aptos

Creek

Aptos Creek Road

FOREST OF NISENE MARKS STATE PARK RIDE #3

Getting There

Take Highway 1 to the Seacliff Beach/Aptos exit. Follow State Beach Road north .25 mile to Soquel Drive and turn right. Continue .5 mile to Aptos Creek Road, turn left, and park at the turnout on the right past the railroad tracks.

Ride #1

Begin pedaling .8 mile up a paved road that turns into dirt for another 2.2 miles to Porter Family Picnic area. This is an excellent resting point for those desiring a more leisurely trip. Continue another .7 mile on the fire road to the Loma Prieta Mill site with remains of the old mill foundation and mill pond. From the mill site it is another .8 mile to Aptos Creek, where the road will begin to climb in earnest; those wishing to keep their ride easy will want to turn around here.

At Aptos Creek the road climbs from 380 to 962 feet in about 1.5 miles, cresting atop China Ridge. Continue climbing at a more gradual pace approximately 3 miles to Sand Point Overlook and an elevation of 1,600 feet. Enjoy the view from the best vantage point in the park, with vistas of Santa Cruz, Monterey Bay, U.C. Santa Cruz, and Ben Lomond Ridge. After you have rested, return the way you came. Be sure to stay to the right and control your speed.

Ride #2

Begin Ride #2 from the Sand Point Overlook. Bear left downhill to West Ridge Trail Camp, approximately .5 mile and 150 feet of elevation loss. Continue down on the Hinkley Fire Road to the gate .9 mile from the trail camp. Watch out for multiple cross drainages that will bury your front wheel and introduce your face to a nearby tree. Hint: keep your weight over the back wheel and keep a relaxed grip on the handlebars.

From the gate ride .2 mile to an intersection, where you will bear right. Pedal .3 mile to another intersection, where you will once again bear to the right. Notice the signs indicating private property. Please respect the owner's privacy. From here the ride goes through a series of three stream crossings that are guaranteed to wet your feet and bring a smile to your face. Continue .4 mile downhill to Olive Springs Road, where you will turn left past a small weight station. Ride 1.2 miles along a scenic and rural road to a left turn on Soquel–San Jose Road. Riders are reminded to use extreme caution due to heavy traffic. Soquel–San Jose Road will take you down to the intersection with Soquel Drive and the town of Soquel. Turn left on Soquel Drive and an easy 3.5-mile pedal back to the parking area and your car.

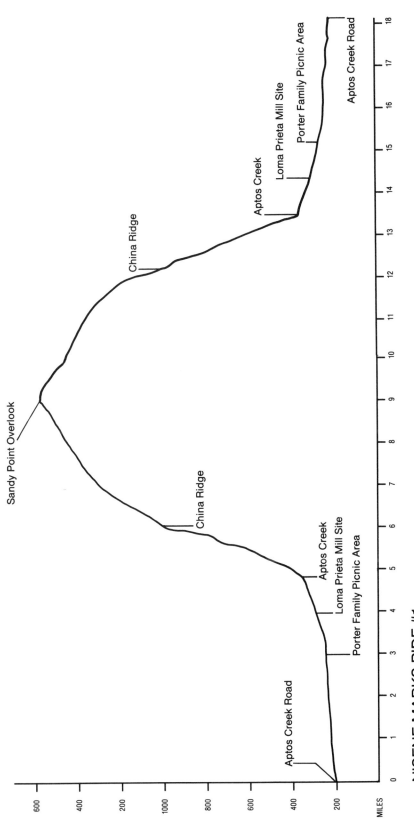

NISENE MARKS RIDE #1

NISENE MARKS RIDE #2

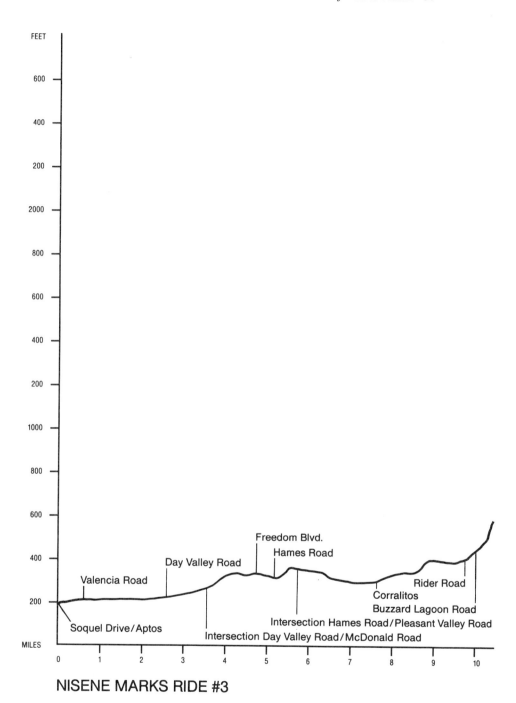

FEET

600

400

200

2000

800

600

400

200

1000

800

600

Freedom Blvd.

Hames Road

400

Day Valley Road

Valencia Road

Rider Road

Corralitos

200

Buzzard Lagoon Road

Soquel Drive/Aptos

Intersection Hames Road/Pleasant Valley Road

Intersection Day Valley Road/McDonald Road

MILES

0   1   2   3   4   5   6   7   8   9   10

NISENE MARKS RIDE #3

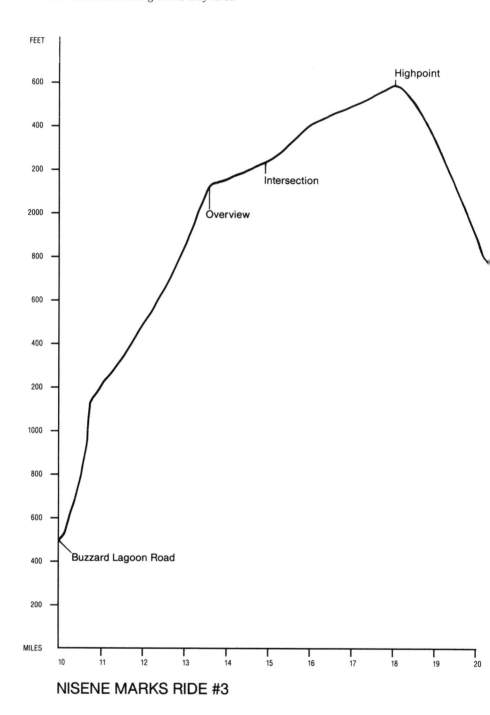

FEET

600

400

200

2000

800

600

400

200

1000

800

600

400

200

MILES

Highpoint

Intersection

Overview

Buzzard Lagoon Road

10   11   12   13   14   15   16   17   18   19   20

NISENE MARKS RIDE #3

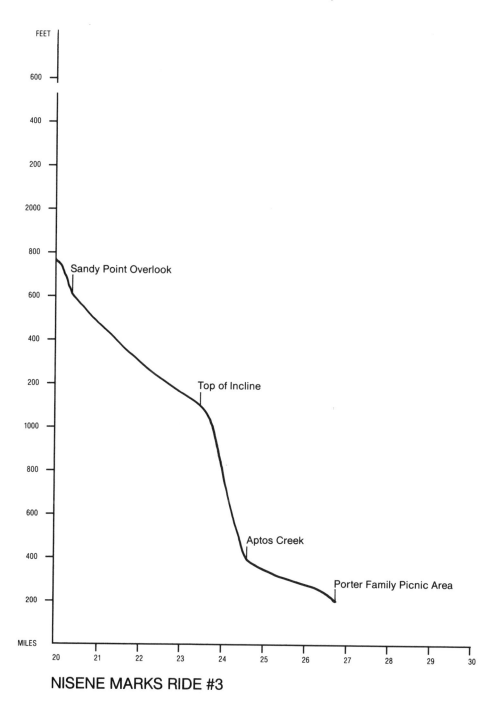

FEET

600

400

200

2000

800

Sandy Point Overlook

600

400

200

Top of Incline

1000

800

600

Aptos Creek

400

Porter Family Picnic Area

200

MILES

20   21   22   23   24   25   26   27   28   29   30

NISENE MARKS RIDE #3

Ride #3

Begin Ride #3 at the turnout and your car. Turn left (east) on Soquel Drive. Ride .1 mile to Trout Gulch Road and turn left. Continue .5 mile to Valencia Road, turn right and pedal 2.6 miles to Day Valley Road. Turn right again and climb gradually through open fields and farmland .8 mile to the intersection of McDonald and Day Valley roads. Stay to the left and cycle 1.3 miles to Freedom Boulevard (use caution on this heavily used road) and Day Valley Road intersection. Turn left and pedal .2 mile on Freedom Boulevard to Hames Road and a short uphill climb.

Following the climb, the road begins to descend .7 mile to the intersection of Pleasant Valley and Hames roads. Bear left and remain on Hames Road for an easy .2-mile descent. The road levels and you will continue for another 1.5 miles to a left turn on Eureka Canyon Road and the town of Corralitos.

Take advantage of the store for a cool drink and a snack if your body requests refueling. From here the road climbs and rolls gently 2.2 miles to Rider Road and Eureka Canyon intersection. Turn left on Rider Road and pedal approximately .3 mile to Buzzard Lagoon Road. Buzzard Lagoon Road climbs steadily, changing to dirt half way up, until reaching the overview at 3.5 miles and an approximate elevation of 2,132 feet. Continue to the Buzzard Lagoon/Aptos Creek Fire Road intersection at 1.3 miles. Bear left on Aptos Creek Fire Road 1 mile to a locked gate. Lift your bike over and continue climbing .8 mile to the highest point in Nisene Marks. Enjoy the view and catch your breath. From the overview it is all downhill to your car via the Sandy Point Overlook. Losing 2,300 feet in just under 12 miles will paste a smile on your face for sure. Please use caution, however, as many others are using the trail for hiking, biking, and playing. CONTROL YOUR SPEED! Word to the wise: Ride #3 covers approximately 29 miles total. Do not try this ride unless you are in very good shape and plan on starting early in the day.

Chapter Nine
HENRY COE STATE PARK

TOPO: *Mississippi Creek 7.5'; Mt. Sizer 7.5'*
RIDE #1: *Beginner and Above*
MILEAGE: *5*
RIDE #2: *Advanced Only!*
MILEAGE: *21.8*
RIDE #3: *Intermediate and Above*
MILEAGE: *14.6*

Description

Essentially a wilderness park, this 67,000-acre preserve is a hidden gem in the San Francisco Bay area. With elevations ranging from 800 to 3,500 feet, the hills offer mixed grassland, oak and pine forests, and deep canyons. Small lakes, streams and a reservoir provide much-needed water for the abundant wildlife. Deer, raccoon, skunks, fox, bobcat, wild turkeys, and the occasional mountain lion all make their home within the park's boundaries. Fall colors and spring wildflowers make these the best seasons to visit the park. The summers are hot and dry and winters often wet with frequent frost and some snow.

Unfortunately, little is known about the original inhabitants who frequented the area thousands of years before the arrival of Spanish explorers in the 18th century. Several camps or village sites of the Costanoan Indians have been discovered within the boundaries of the park. More recently, 1776 to be exact, Juan Bautista de Anza named the major creek in the area Arroyo del Coyote; this has since been changed to Coyote Creek. American influence in the valley came during 1846 in the form of cattle ranching and wheat growing.

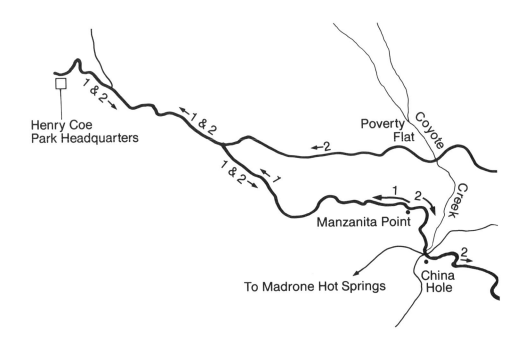

Henry Coe
Park Headquarters

Poverty
Flat

Manzanita Point

To Madrone Hot Springs

China
Hole

HENRY COE STATE PARK
RIDE #1 & #2

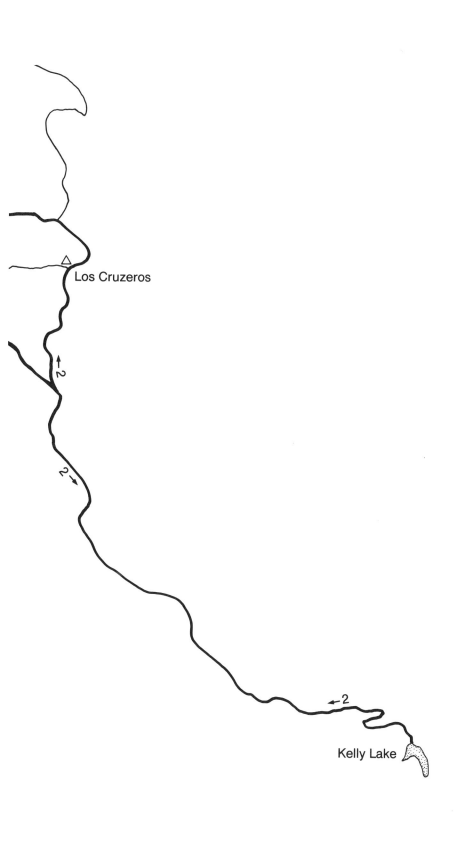

Los Cruzeros

2

2

2

Kelly Lake

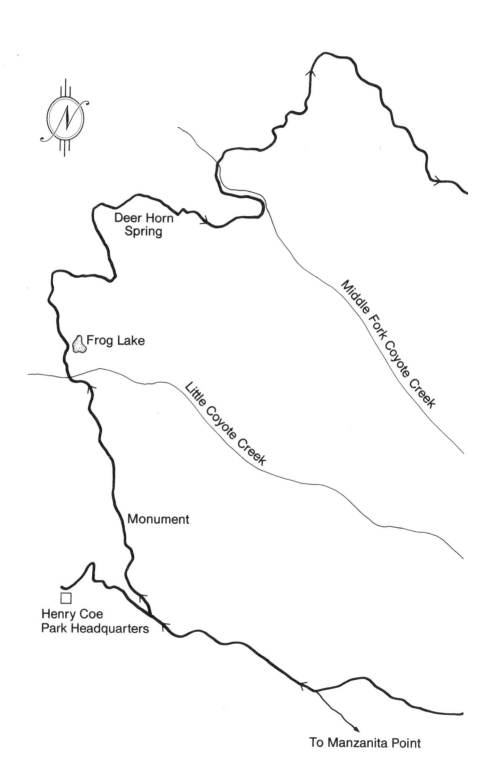

Deer Horn
Spring

Middle Fork Coyote Creek

Frog Lake

Little Coyote Creek

Monument

Henry Coe
Park Headquarters

To Manzanita Point

HENRY COE STATE PARK
RIDE #3

△ Mt. Sizer

Poverty
Flat

When the railroad was added to the valley, fruit growing began to replace wheat and cattle so the ranchers moved higher into the hills. Through many transformations, the land became a county park in 1953 and later a state park in 1958 with the donation of Pine Ridge Ranch by the daughter of original homesteader Henry Coe. It was Sada Sutcliffe Coe's wish that the park provide "peace for one's soul and food for the power of thought." We think that you will find, no matter what your venture, the peace that she wished.

Getting There
From Highway 101 take the East Dunne Avenue exit bearing east at Morgan Hill. Follow the signs up a narrow, winding 13-mile road past Anderson Reservoir to its dead end at the park headquarters.

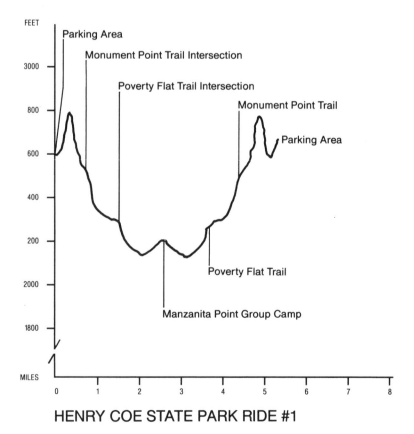

HENRY COE STATE PARK RIDE #1

The Ride
Much of the park is remote wilderness. Trails and roads are steep, rocky, and sometimes treacherous. Caution is the word and control is the key. We feel that only one ride is suitable for beginners, with the remainder ideal for strong intermediates and above. In terms of beauty and solitude this park rates as one of our favorites. It is that solitude that merits any rider be prepared for the unexpected. Two water bottles and a water purification system are essential. Springs and streams are abundant in the park, but the water must be treated before drinking. A basic tool kit and small first-aid kit are strongly recommended (see appendix for listing of contents). For maximum enjoyment start early in the day and plan your turnaround to coincide with a time, not a destination. There are several wilderness campsites in the park available to bikers, call the park headquarters for information at 408-779-2728.

Ride #1
This is the only ride suitable for beginners. We would recommend bringing a picnic lunch and enjoying the solitude and view to be had at Manzanita Group Camp. From the park headquarters, ride through the gate and up a fairly easy incline, gaining 200 feet toward Manzanita Point and Poverty Flat. At .6 mile, Monument Road branches off to the left (Ride #3 begins here and continues up towards the Monument and Frog Lake). Continue straight and downhill to the intersection with Poverty Flat and Manzanita Point fire roads at 1.5 miles. Stay right, continuing on a rolling road to the sign for China Hole Trail (Ride #2 description starts here). Bear left and pedal several hundred yards to the turnaround at the trailhead for Rabbit Spring and the farthest point in Manzanita Group Camp. The mileage to this point is 2.5. Enjoy the views and your lunch and then return the way you came. Round-trip mileage is approximately 5 miles.

Ride #2
Beginning at Manzanita Group Camp and the cutoff for China Hole, head straight and down the single-track trail toward China Hole. The ride is spectacular, with super views into the Coyote Creek Canyon. Watch your speed carefully; the trail descends 1,000 feet in approximately 1.4 miles and several very tight switchbacks require some strong downhill skills. Take a well-deserved break at Coyote Creek (the best swimming hole in the park) before beginning the steep climb up to Mahoney Meadows.

The trail is somewhat confusing here; the route is found directly across the creek heading up and mostly east. You will now be paying your dues for the wonderful descent to China Hole as the trail rapidly winds and climbs approximately 800 feet in 1.3 miles. Catch your breath at the in-

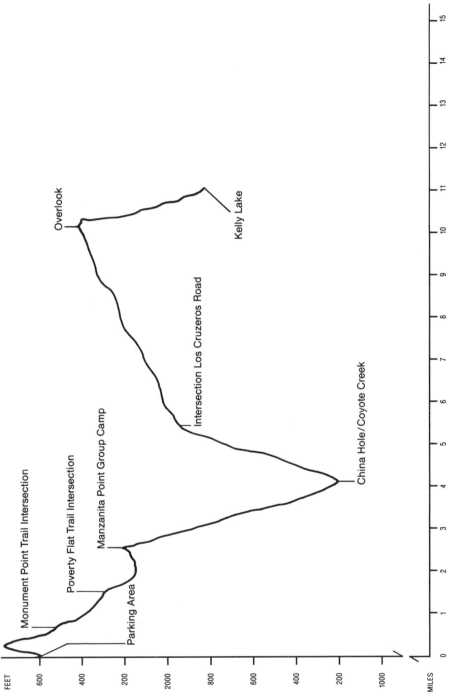

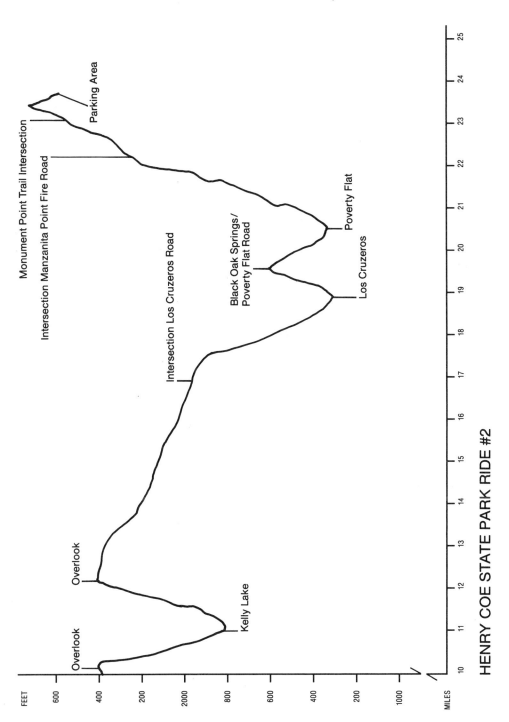

Monument Point Trail Intersection

Intersection Manzanita Point Fire Road

Parking Area

Intersection Los Cruzeros Road

Black Oak Springs/
Poverty Flat Road

Poverty Flat

Los Cruzeros

Overlook

Overlook

Kelly Lake

FEET

600

400

2000

800

600

400

200

1000

MILES

10 11 12 13 14 15 16 17 18 19 20 21 22 23 24 25

HENRY COE STATE PARK RIDE #2

tersection with the fire road leading north to Lost Spring and Los Cruzeros and south to Kelly Lake. Bear to the right; though gradual, the trail rolls and climbs 4.7 miles, gaining approximately 600 feet to a peak elevation of 2,400 feet. Several intersections will be encountered; stay to the left, passing by the cutoffs for Coit Camp and another unsigned fire road. Spend a few moments enjoying the vista before descending .7 mile to Kelly Lake and an elevation loss of 600 feet.

Once at Kelly Lake you have several options. Our guided route retraces your ride to the intersection with China Hole and the fire road to Los Cruzeros. However, if you are still feeling strong and it is early in the day, you may opt to follow a route along Willow Ridge, passing by Coit Lake, Hoover Lake, and descending the Willow Ridge Trail to Los Cruzeros, where you will once again join our guided ride. We will leave you to your sense of adventure on this one.

Continue straight after retracing your path to the intersection of China Hole and Los Cruzeros Fire Road. The route descends rapidly to the valley floor over .9 mile of steep and sometimes very rutted road. Once at Los Cruzeros the trail climbs steeply .4 mile to its intersection with the Fire Road to Black Oak Springs and Poverty Flat (Ride #3 joins us here for the conclusion of its tour). Bear left to Poverty Flat and a fun 1.2-mile descent. Once at Poverty Flat enjoy a well-earned rest and restock your water bottles from the creek, if you brought water purification equipment. From here the path crosses the stream and begins a mind-bending climb, gaining 1,000 feet in just under 1.8 miles to the intersection with the fire road to Manzanita Group Camp. It's homeward bound from here over a fairly level 1.5 miles back to your car. Still smiling? Good, so were we.

Ride #3
Beginning at the Monument cutoff from Ride #1, climb approximately 400 feet in .5 mile to the Monument and intersection with a hiking trail branching off to the left. Continue straight toward Frog Lake. The road descends about 600 feet over the next mile until leveling out at the lake. From here the fire road follows a rolling track (climbing and dropping 200 feet) 1.3 miles to Deer Horn Springs. Lower your seat and prepare for a wild and woolly 800-foot elevation loss in one mile bringing you to the cutoff for Upper Camp.

Raise your seat and brace yourself for some serious mountain bike walking—straight up Short Cut Road to Blue Ridge Fire Road and the turnoff for Mt. Sizer. Once at the top, look back. You have just walked your bike up about 1,500 feet in just under 1.3 miles. Bear right and continue for approximately 1 mile and the intersection with the Mt. Sizer trail; it is worth the short pedal to the top of the 3,200-foot summit, one of the

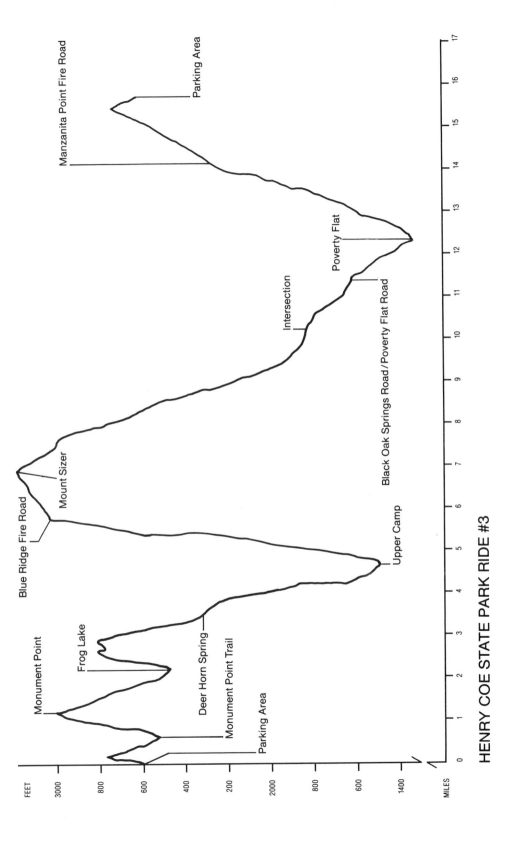

HENRY COE STATE PARK RIDE #3

highest points in the park. Pedal on for .7 mile over relatively level terrain with spectacular vistas to the north and south. The trail begins to descend gradually, losing 1,600 feet over the next 2.6 miles until reaching the intersection with Los Cruzeros to the left (east) and Poverty Flat up and to the west. Consult Ride #2 for trail description through Poverty Flat and back to your car.

Chapter Ten

JOSEPH D. GRANT RANCH COUNTY PARK

TOPO: *Lick Observatory 7.5'; Mt. Day 7.5'*
RIDE #1: *Beginner and Above*
MILEAGE: *2.5*
RIDE #2: *Intermediate and Above*
MILEAGE: *9.6*
RIDE #3: *Advanced Beginner and Above*
MILEAGE: *8.5*

Description

Joseph D. Grant County Park is a frequently overlooked jewel within Santa Clara County. Though livestock grazing takes place on much of the park, there is ample room for hikers, equestrians, and, of course, mountain bikers. The park is located in the Mt. Hamilton range very near the Lick Observatory. The landscape is rich and colorful with rolling grasslands, magnificent oak woodlands, and spectacular vistas of the surrounding mountains. Lush and green in the spring or golden and subtle in the fall, this park is worth experiencing. Keep a careful eye open for wildlife as you pedal along and you just might be rewarded with a view of a golden eagle hunting the fields or a bobcat melting into the shadows.

Getting There

Just south of the 280/880 interchange on 101 take the Tully Road exit heading east. Stay on Tully until you reach Quimby Road and turn right. Quimby Road narrows just before heading into the foothills and winds approximately 4 miles until the intersection with Mt. Hamilton Road. At Mt. Hamilton Road bear right and you will see the park entrance in ap-

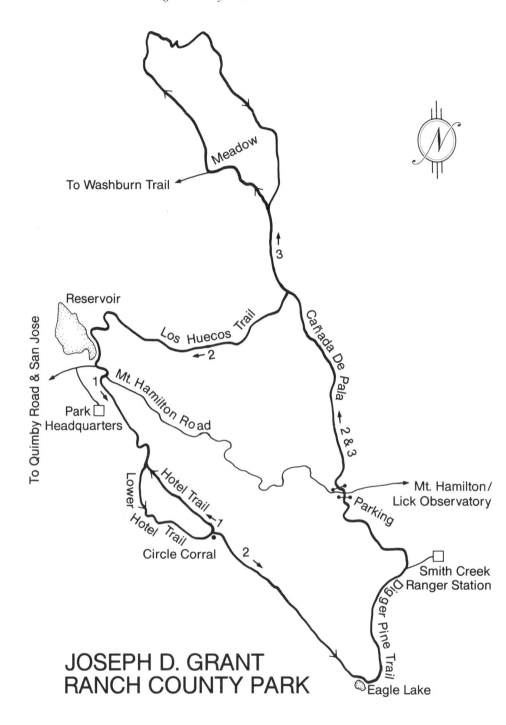

To Washburn Trail

Meadow

Reservoir

To Quimby Road & San Jose

Los Huecos Trail

Cañada De Pala

Mt. Hamilton Road

Park Headquarters

Lower Hotel Trail

Hotel Trail

Circle Corral

Parking

Mt. Hamilton / Lick Observatory

Smith Creek Ranger Station

Digger Pine Trail

Eagle Lake

JOSEPH D. GRANT
RANCH COUNTY PARK

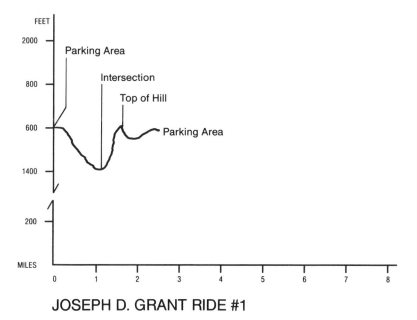

JOSEPH D. GRANT RIDE #1

proximately .25 mile on your right. For Rides #1 and #2 you will enter the park and leave your car near the visitor center. For Ride #3 you will continue driving 3.5 miles up Mt. Hamilton Road to a dirt parking area next to the road and the trailhead for the Bohnhoff and Canada De Pala trails. Please note that if you have never ridden in the park before you are required to sign a waiver and register yourself at the visitor center before using the trails with your mountain bike. It is also important to remember that these trails are used by everyone and you as a responsible mountain biker must yield the right-of-way to pedestrians and equestrians.

Ride #1

Beginning at the visitor center parking area, go east through two livestock gates and the start of the Hotel Trail. The Lower Hotel and Hotel trails form a 2.5-mile loop that is well suited for beginners. Approximately .2 mile from the last gate bear right on the Lower Hotel Trail along the corral fence. The trail descends gradually 1 mile until meeting up once again with the Upper Hotel Trail at the Circle Corral. (Ride #2, for intermediate-to-advanced riders, continues right, climbing the Hotel Trail to Eagle Lake.) Bear left on Hotel Trail for an elevation gain of 160 feet in .75 mile. At the top of the hill you have an option of taking a side trip to Bass Lake, a decision we will leave up to your sense of adventure. Hotel Trail descends 160 feet in .25 mile from the hilltop and rejoins the main trail for the return to the parking area.

Ride #2

Follow the trail description for Ride #1 until the Circle Corral. This ride has very steep ascents and challenging descents, making it suitable only for intermediate-to-advanced riders. You are guaranteed to feel your pulse on this one, and walking is to be expected.

From Circle Corral bear right into the trees, where the trail immediately begins to climb. From this point you will gain 680 feet in 1.75 miles to Eagle Lake. It is every bit as hard as it sounds as the dirt is loose and rutted. There are several flat sections in between the climbs — not enough to catch your breath, but just long enough to give you hope.

At Eagle Lake take time to have lunch; it is a beautiful spot with excellent vistas among the oaks. If you are fatigued or looking to make this a short trip, head back the way you came, controlling speed, to the parking area.

JOSEPH D. GRANT RIDE #2

Continuing on, head left at Eagle Lake, where the trail makes a quick, but short 160-foot descent into a cool canyon. Following the stream bed for a brief period, the Digger Pine Trail (named for the stand of Digger Pines you pass near the crest of the ridge) becomes quite rocky with a number of short, but intense ascents. One mile from Eagle Lake turn left on the Bohnhoff Trail for yet another steep ascent. (We didn't even bat an eye and walked this one.)

After about a 400-foot elevation gain, the trail levels out quickly and meanders along the ridge before making a quick descent to Mt. Hamilton Road, .8 mile from Digger Pine. There is a gate on either side of the road, please be sure to secure them. You are now on the Canada De Pala Trail, heading north. The trail immediately tests your legs as it climbs 200 feet in approximately .2 mile. Once you reach the top of the ridge, your efforts are rewarded with 360 degree views of the surrounding foothills.

The trail continues another rolling 1.5 miles along the ridge until the intersection with Los Huecos Trail. (Ride #3 will continue straight along the Canada De Pala Trail at this point.) Turn left for a wild and woolly 1.7-mile descent, losing 840 feet to the reservoir. Use caution: half way down, after a short uphill and in a somewhat flat area, you will encounter a barbed wire fence that requires opening a gate or lifting your bike over. After reaching the lake, turn left to Mt. Hamilton Road. At the road bear left and in approximately .1 mile turn right, through a gate, and head .3 mile back to the parking area. Congratulations! You have just completed a 9.6-mile loop.

Ride #3
Approximately 3.5 miles from the main park gate on Mt. Hamilton Road you come to a dirt parking area on the right side of the road. From here cross over the road (to the north side) and through the gate to begin the ride. This tour is suitable for advanced beginners all the way to experienced riders. Follow the directions for Ride #2 beginning at Mt. Hamilton Road to the Los Huecos Trail. At the Los Huecos Trail continue straight on Canada De Pala, losing 180 feet in .8 mile to the Halls Valley Trail. From here you will gain 200 feet in .4 mile to the intersection of Canada De Pala and Pala Seca Trail. Bear left, continuing on Canada De Pala, which remains fairly flat with a slight descent into a wonderful meadow.

After .6 mile the trail meets with the Washburn Trail (illegal for bikes) and continues right, along the border of the meadow. The next 1 mile parallels a stream for a wonderfully cool and refreshing canyon ride. All too soon, however, the trail leaves the shade and climbs approximately 100 feet to a line shack used when herding cattle. At the shack bear right along a faint trail. You are now on the Pala Seca Trail, which climbs steeply

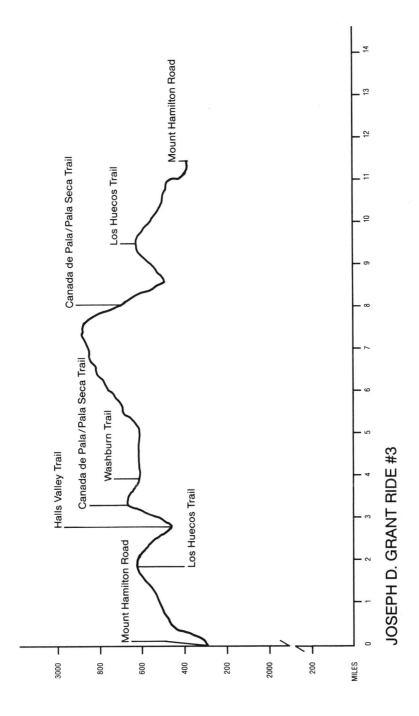

JOSEPH D. GRANT RIDE #3

200 feet to the top of the ridge, giving one the feeling of being on top of the world.

From the line shack back to the Canada De Pala trail is 2.1 miles. The descent from the ridge to the intersection is rapid and steep, but not too difficult. Once back on the Canada De Pala Trail, turn left and retrace your path to Mt. Hamilton Road gate and parking area.

Chapter Eleven
SAN FRANCISCO BAY
NATIONAL WILDLIFE REFUGE

TOPO: *Mountain View 7.5'; Newark 7.5'*
RIDE #1: *Beginner and Above*
MILEAGE: *5 miles with option for adding a .7-mile loop.*
RIDE #2: *Beginner and Above*
MILEAGE: *8.7*

Description

Established in 1972, this 23,000-acre wildlife refuge is easily overlooked while speeding by on the local freeways. Those who are willing to take the time to pedal along the levees and shorelines will discover a city-bounded wilderness teeming with life. Birds are perhaps the most obvious denizens, with over 250 species using this habitat during the course of of a year, most abundantly during the fall and winter. Given time and patience, one may also view a hidden world of striped bass, crabs, harbor seals, and even the occasional otter. It might be of interest to you, as it was to us, that acre for acre, salt water marshes out-produce our best farms for nutrients. These marshes are not wastelands as they are often viewed. It is worth your time to take a peek, but remember to keep your eyes and ears peeled.

Getting There

Visitor Headquarters in Fremont: From Highway 84 near 880 take the Thornton Avenue exit south toward Newark. Turn right on Marshland Road and continue approximately .25 mile to a right turn into the visitor center parking area. Now follow the directions for Ride #1 outlined below.

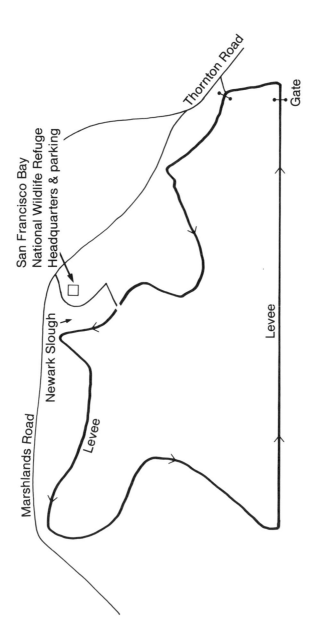

SAN FRANCISCO BAY NATIONAL WILDLIFE REFUGE
RIDE #1

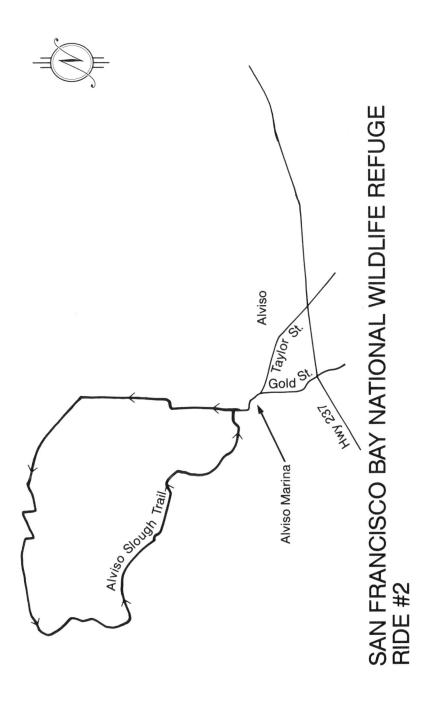

SAN FRANCISCO BAY NATIONAL WILDLIFE REFUGE
RIDE #2

Alviso Entrance: From Highway 237, east of 880 and north of 101, take the North First Street exit and head north. Bear right on Gold Street and drive two blocks until making a left turn on Elizabeth Street. Drive two blocks on Elizabeth, then make a right turn on Hope Street, which will take you into the trailhead parking area. It can get somewhat confusing in here, but your ultimate goal is the Alviso Marina parking area. Stay alert and you will get there. Now follow the directions for Ride #2.

Ride #1

Though this ride definitely has a beginner level of difficulty, the area's abundant wildlife and serenity provide enjoyment for all riders. There are two trails to ride in this part of the refuge. Starting and finishing at the visitor center, the Tidelands Walking Trail completes a .7-mile loop with one minor hill. There are walkers and birders present, so watch your speed.

The second trail, called the Newark Slough Trail, begins just below the visitor center across a wooden access bridge. This trail is a very flat and easy 5-mile loop through the Newark Slough and affords the visitor numerous opportunities to view birds, sea life, and mammals that frequent the area.

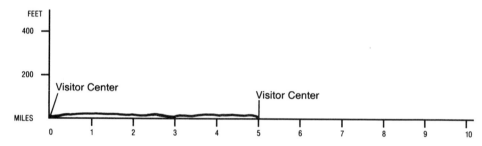

SAN FRANCISCO BAY WILDLIFE REFUGE RIDE #1

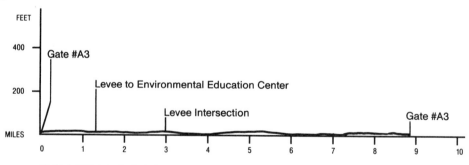

SAN FRANCISCO BAY WILDLIFE REFUGE RIDE #2

Ride #2

Beginning at gate #A3, you will head out onto the Alviso Slough Trail for an 8.7-mile loop that will end back at this gate. Don't be turned off by the industrial appearance; the terrain will improve within 1.4 miles to that of a true saltwater marsh. At 1.4 miles, a levee veers off to the right and will take you to the Environmental Education Center, which is not open to the public. For the purpose of our ride you will continue north. At 3 miles a levee branches off to the left; this levee rejoins the main trail 1.2 miles north of the parking area and is an option to shorten your ride if you wish. From here just follow the trail through open slough, mud flats, and saltwater marsh back to the parking area and a finishing mileage of 8.7. Birders, casual or otherwise, won't want to leave their binoculars or birding books behind on this ride.

Chapter Twelve
COYOTE HILLS REGIONAL PARK

TOPO: *Newark 7.5'*
THE RIDE: *Beginner and Above*
MILEAGE: *8.6 miles with an option to add 2.6 or 1.4 additional miles*

Description

Coyote Hills is a 1,039-acre wildlife sanctuary located at the south end of San Francisco Bay near Fremont. This area has an extensive history dating back almost 2,300 years. The diet of the Indians living on this land consisted of mostly shellfish, evidenced by the four shell mounds visible today. In addition to its rich history, the park's resources include grassy hills, freshwater marshes, and seasonal wetlands. During migration and in the winter this area becomes a bird-watcher's paradise. Don't forget, this park is a wildlife sanctuary, so please keep to the trails and leave everything as you found it. Although the rides in this refuge are mostly flat and easy, we feel the scenic beauty will appeal to all levels of bikers. We recommend an early morning visit to take advantage of smaller crowds, cooler temperatures, and more visible wildlife.

Getting There

Just west of Highway 84 and Interstate 880 lies Coyote Hills. Take the Ardenwood Boulevard exit off of Highway 84 and head north. Turn left on Commerce Avenue and drive through the Ardenwood Technology Park, past Paseo Padre Parkway and continue on Patterson Ranch Road to the Park entrance and the dirt parking directly following.

The Ride

From the parking area and the information kiosk, ride .5 mile on the bike

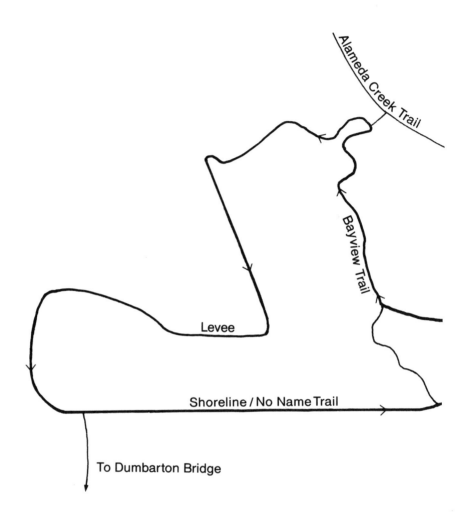

Alameda Creek Trail

Bayview Trail

Levee

Shoreline / No Name Trail

To Dumbarton Bridge

COYOTE HILLS REGIONAL PARK

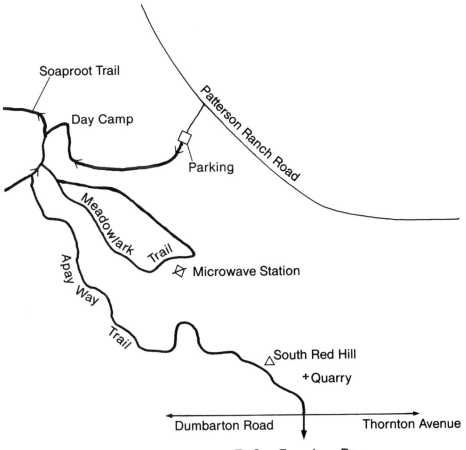

Soaproot Trail

Day Camp

Patterson Ranch Road

Parking

Meadowlark Trail

Apay Way Trail

Microwave Station

South Red Hill

+ Quarry

Dumbarton Road   Thornton Avenue

To San Francisco Bay
National Wildlife Refuge

path paralleling Patterson Ranch Road. Turn left at the Alameda Creek Ponding Area and head toward the Day Camp and Quarry on the Bayview Trail. At the Day Camp, the trail makes a sharp hairpin. Head west (left) immediately after the hairpin on the Soaproot Trail, which becomes a dirt road and climbs steeply until its crest and intersection with the Hill Trail (illegal for mountain bikes).

You will quickly lose elevation until your abrupt rejoining of the Bayview Trail (watch your speed). Turn right on the Bayview Trail and continue until meeting up with the Alameda Creek Trail. You have gone 2.3 miles to here and may turn back to the parking area by bearing right on the Bayview Trail.

For those continuing on, head left and onto the sand levee of the Alameda Creek Trail/Shoreline Trail. At 5.8 miles the path turns into No Name Trail. Dumbarton Bridge Trail branches right (to the south) and intersects with Marshlands Road if you are feeling adventurous. Otherwise, continue on the No Name Trail until you once again rejoin the Bayview Trail at 7.2 miles. Follow the Bayview Trail to Patterson Ranch Road and your car with an ending mileage of approximately 8.6.

If you wish to add distance and, of course, scenic beauty, we recommend riding up and back on Apay Way Trail (2.6 miles) and/or Meadowlark Trail Loop (1.4 miles). Apay Way Trail is fairly flat dirt road with a gradual incline during the first .4 mile. The turnaround point is the information booth at the bridge crossing Highway 84. Should you wish to extend your ride even farther, it is possible to ride over the bridge and tour the San Francisco Bay National Wildlife Refuge. (See Chapter Eleven for more detailed information). Meadowlark Trail is not for the faint of heart; the first .6 mile climbs very steeply to a microwave station. You will have just enough time to catch your breath before a rapid descent to the marsh and a rejoining with Bayview Trail at 1.4 miles.

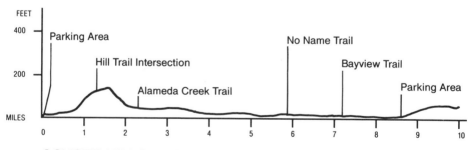

COYOTE HILLS REGIONAL PARK

Cycling Necessities

TIRE IRONS
PATCH KIT
SPARE TUBE
TIRE PUMP
CHAIN TOOL
APPROPRIATE SELECTION OF ALLEN WRENCHES: check with
  bike shop
SPOKE WRENCH
SPARE SPOKES: for your wheel type, these can be taped to the chain stay
CHANGE: for a phone call or other purchases
FIRST AID KIT: assorted bandaids, Ace bandage, 3 × 3 gauze pads, adhe-
  sive tape, moleskin, aspirin, antiseptic, tincture of Benzoin, needle, mat-
  ches, sunscreen, water purification tablets
WATER BOTTLE: your body needs a minimum of 2 quarts of fluid per day,
  so plan accordingly!
COMPASS
SMALL LIGHT: flashlight, headlamp, or bike light
HIGH-ENERGY MUNCHIES: gorp, nuts, cheese, dried fruit

For an overnight trip add the following items:
MOUNTAIN BIKE REAR PANNIER RACK: even if you are opting not to
  use panniers, the rack gives you a surface to which to attach your tent and
  sleeping bag and also minimizes the inevitable brown racing strip on your
  back in wet and muddy terrain
SMALL BIKE PANNIERS AND/OR LARGE FANNY PACK: use what-
  ever system maintains optimum agility and balance
SMALL STOVE AND FUEL
COMPACT COOKING POT, 1 TO 2 QUARTS
COMPACT AND LIGHTWEIGHT DOWN SLEEPING BAG

COMPACT AND LIGHTWEIGHT TENT/BIVI SACK
SMALL KNIFE
SMALL SPOON: for eating and stirring
WATERPROOF/WINDPROOF MATCHES

The Well-Dressed Rider

CYCLING GLOVES: well padded and ventilated

RIDING SHORTS: comfy, nonchafing, snug fitting, and quick drying

STIFF-SOLED SHOES: must be easy to pull out of toe-clips and useable for hiking

SUNGLASSES: retainers are recommended lest you and your glasses part company on the first significant bump

T-SHIRT

HELMET! Skid lids are out! Hard plastic shell and foam liner are recommended

WINDBREAKER/GORTEX RAINWEAR

THERMAL UNDERWEAR: capilene, polypro, or silk for cold weather.

WOOL OR SYNCHILLA/POLAR FLEECE HAT: for times when your helmet is off and your head is cold

This is not an all-inclusive listing. You may want to add or delete items depending on your personal and weather-dictated needs.

Overnight Accommodations

The following areas offer overnight car and tent camping facilities.
Reservations are advised.

Grant Ranch County Park
Henry Cowell State Park
Butano State Park
Big Basin State Park

To make reservations at any California State Park call MISTIX
1-800-444-7275.

Rider's Responsibility

At the time of publication, all of the rides described within these pages were legal. However, due to political pressures, environmental damage, and other mitigating circumstances, any trail may be closed at any time. Please, plan your trip carefully and call ahead to the appropriate agency to determine legality of trails and conditions of their use. Even if described in this book, do not ride on a trail that has been closed to use.

PORTOLA STATE PARK
Star Route 2
La Honda, CA 94020
(415) 948-9098

BIG BASIN STATE PARK
21600 Big Basin Way
Boulder Creek, CA 95006
(408) 338-6132

BUTANO STATE PARK
PO. Box 9
Pescadero, CA 94060
(415) 879-0173

NISENE MARKS STATE PARK
%101 North Big Trees Park Rd.
Felton, CA 95018
(408) 335-4598

HENRY COWELL STATE PARK
101 North Big Trees Park Rd.
Felton, CA 95018
(408) 335-4598

COYOTE HILLS REGIONAL PARK
11500 Skyline Blvd.
Oakland, CA 94619
(415) 531-9300

SAN FRANCISCO NATIONAL WILDLIFE REFUGE
P.O. Box 524
Newark, CA 94560
(415) 792-0222

GRANT RANCH COUNTY PARK
298 Garden Hill Drive
Los Gatos, CA 95030
(408) 358-3741

HENRY COE STATE PARK
P.O. Box 846
Morgan Hill, CA 95037
(408) 779-2728

MIDPENINSULA OPEN SPACE DISTRICT
Old Mill Office Center, Bldg. C, Suite 135, 201 San Antonio Circle
Mountain View, CA 94040
(415) 949-5500

Much research and effort has gone into making this guide the best it can
be, however we welcome reader input on improvements. If you find an
inaccuracy or if you have a favorite ride you'd like to share, please drop
us a line.

Michael Hodgson and Mark Lord
c/o Western Tanager Press
1111 Pacific Avenue
Santa Cruz, CA 95060

ABOUT THE AUTHORS

MICHAEL HODGSON is a free-lance writer and author living in the Bay Area. The wilderness has been part of his life since early childhood. An experienced cross-country ski instructor, mountaineer, and mountain biker, Michael most enjoys sharing his love for the outdoors, through his writing.

MARK LORD's interests span backcountry ski mountaineering and climbing, ocean kayaking, long-distance cycle touring, and mountain biking. Mark, a resident of the Santa Cruz mountains, has also authored a guide to ski touring at Lake Tahoe and is a free-lance writer and guide.